Yes to it all

by Alan Davison

for more books by Alan Davison, visit his website at:
http://blurtso.com & http://blog.blurtso.com

Shield Publishers

ISBN– 9781070730707

other books by Alan Davison:

Blurtso Goes Around
To Bray or Not to Bray
On Walden Pond
Blurtseau Lundif
Waiting for Blurtsoh
The Adventures of Captain Harvey
Particles
Graham Cracker Crumbs
Ditto Goes to School
Franklin the Goat
The Bug and You and Me
Blurtso el Burro

for my father,
who gave me his love for words,
and for my mother,
who never got to see these poems

Yes to it all

by

Alan Davison

(poems from 1979-2020)

Yes to it all

Wandering

Love Poems

Author's Note

A collection of poems is an incomplete picture. It is
a palette of colors that catch the eye, a series of
sparks on the stream. The loving family and friends,
the fortuitous place and time, the shelter and security,
are the overlooked spaces in between. They are the
foundation beneath the feet. These are the sparks and
colors of an extremely fortunate life.

Alan Davison, May 2020

Before you go

Before you go,
I will tell you what was here.

First, an endless love.

Second, silent
and spoken communication.

Third, any possession
worth working for.

Fourth, imagination and a song.

Now you can choose to stay,
or you can go.

Words

I

If I laid my head on the page,
if I fell asleep between the lines,
maybe my thoughts could flow into words
and all would be ordered, neat and tidy.

Then I could find out how I feel,
and what I have to do.

II

The pen is restless;

if by accident,
if by a slip of the hand
the right words came,
if I caught your smile
in a cage of sound,
then I could touch you,
kiss you, hold you.

III

Words surface breathing,
free like birds,
they blink,
a ray of laughter,
a slip,
tears.
Words grow flowers,
wave in the breeze,
they stretch,
naked,
tenderly alive.

IV

I, like a child,
words, like blocks,
soft ones, hard ones,
awkward ones.
I stack them
 on
    top
       of
          each
              other,
side by side,
    alone,
any way that will make you smile.
And when I finish,
unequal castles
and clumsy towers,
I wait for you.

I hope you'll like our home,
hope you won't knock it down
and make me cry.

V

After the same words,
light, wind, fire,
there is nothing more.
There are only lines,
paper and ink,
and the repetition of repetition.

I can write,
fill the page,
and between margins
try to live,
but it is impossible
to paint your smile,

or create a rose,
with emptiness.

VI

There is only one way
to write a poem.

Pen, paper, silence.

Sounds from the past,
sorted and inflected by the present.

Sounds the stars make.
Sounds the stars hear.
Sights the stars see.

Stars,
seeing, hearing, speaking.

VII

With each word
the structure weakens.

You are soothing,
simple,
no more than a letter,
a sound.

VIII

You can spend your life looking for it,
a line, a word, a shadow
that will remain forever,
and just when you believe you've found it,
the lights go out and all is black, erased.

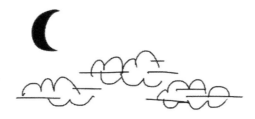

He was

He was romantic from the start.

Weaned on Yeats, Eliot, and Neruda.

He was addicted to the flight and fall.

He believed in adrenaline.

He carried believers along with him
and they carried him.

It was exhausting, and required
long draughts of recuperative solitude.

He didn't have an Irish constitution.

He was the life of the party
and a recluse.

Eventually simple, natural things
filled his solitude.

He had no need
to conquer situations or mountains.

But he still loved the flight and fall.

New light

Cézanne painted the same mountain
again and again,
attempting to catch in colors
the changing mornings and afternoons
on the white canvas page.

In like fashion the poet
writes the same poem, again and again,
sketching the changing contours
of the day's hills and valleys
on the page.

Nothing new under the sun,
except the sun's changing light
making everything new.

Ambition

The young boy tosses a rubber ball
against a brick wall,
over and over.

The skier skis, alone,
beneath the snow-heavy pines.

The musician strums her guitar
and sings her songs
to the night.

Love of doing
brings love of doing.

The rest is advertisement,
self-promotion, propaganda.

Fertile limit

You hold your sword
over me,
never out of mind,
waiting
for the end
that is certain to come.
You are the sad but not evil
mother of vitality,
the threat of mortality
that creates
the electric moment,
the edge that threatens
and gives meaning.

You are the mother of the thought
that this time,
or any time,
may be the last time.

You make every time
the only time.

I push you to the back
with duties, dreams, and routines,
but you are never forgotten,
you are ever-giving, ever-inciting,
forever creating fire and flavor
with fear.

I'm in no hurry to meet you,
but I'm glad you're here.

Stepping out

Every interesting thought I've had,
was born in laziness.

The river rushes,
its light flashes on the eyes,
the tongues of water
splash the ears.

Riding the river
is food for thought,
but it's impossible to observe the river
from within the river.

Mirror

When I don't look in the mirror,
I'm certain
I look like a valley, a mountain, or a tree.

I don't doubt
I am the flowers in that field,
the river on that hill.

My clouds never grow thin.

My soil is never wrinkled or rough.

Everywhere I turn
I see a mirror.

Look! There's my smile,
that splash of water on stone!

Desert crossing

I have enough water
to cross the sand.

The friendly sun threatens
to be unfriendly.

My possessions remain at home.
And my friends.

The world is reduced
to sand, sun, and me.

I am grateful to the sand
and sun
for revealing me:
a collection of organs and limbs,
stepping across the sand.

And the sudden joy of freedom
from all that was not me,
from people
and possessions,
is matched only by the joy
of the sound of water
in my canteen.

Why?

I've watched you,
your busy hands putting blocks in order,
and I know you want to believe
that things work out that way,

but I can't tell you why
a car drives on without stopping,
and your dog lies dead in the gutter.

Yes to it all

When the best among us
are assassinated,
when dictators rise to power
on the shoulders
of good people blinded by fear,
when comfort is an excuse
to take more than your share,
when the world wreaks havoc
with storm, flood, and fire
on the unfortunate and defenseless…

Some choose to fight.

When the young mother suffers
the pain of loss,
when the retiree forgets, again,
the name of his spouse,
when the widow reaches at night
for the shape that is not there…

Some ask why.

Some dream of a place
where only half a world exists.

Some smile
the smile of the buddha.

Filings

We are iron filings
drawn in circles
by common magnets.

Occasionally,
we are drawn too close
to other filings,
and we exchange
one magnet for another.

We call the results
careers, families, friends.

Into the unknown

It's frightening
to close your eyes and step.

The earth you know
is not beneath you.

The faces you know
are not seen.

Trusting the unknown on earth
is true religion.

Trusting that there are unknown others,
eager and open-hearted,
waiting to greet you.

All of a sudden,
or in the nick of time,
whenever they are needed
they appear, they always appear,
eager and open-hearted
to greet you.

Candlelight

I

Candlelight,
an intimate breath
closes your eyes,
touches your lips
with the trace of a kiss.
Your hair lies still,
brushed back by fingers,
like a winter waterfall
that catches the light,
splashes circles
on your shoulders.

The stillness grows
and we remain,
timeless, tranquil,
until a car passes,
or a voice echoes,
and we awake.

II

Now that your smile is gone,
now that time has lost
the line of your shoulders,
my fingers have forgotten
the harmony of your hands,
and the stars won't bring me
the light of your eyes,
all that remains is a feeling,
a slow kiss, a feather.

III

It must be you,
the light at the slow river's edge,
your reflection reaching across
to the bank where I sit.

It must be your eyes,
watching the water flow,
that cause the light to ripple and waver,
finding its way to my heart.

I call to you.

Candlelight flickers on the ceiling,
a voice startles me, and I awake.
It must have been you,
silent in the European evening.

I blow out the candles
and go back to sleep.

Journey

I lie down by your side
as if at the side of a transparent pool
that catches and distills
the sparks of night.
You move next to me,
shifting to find the perfect fit
of desire and despair,
and your hungry skin,
skin of shadow and sun,
rises to my touch
that falls, wraps, and descends,
until you draw me in
to the darkness of your light,
to the pink fruit of your mouth,
to the golden canopy
of your hair that shuts out the night.

Beneath your tawny mane
live the origins of light.

Slow river rising,
throbbing stone,
splash, fill,
skin glow
after
summer rain,
give, take,
dripping flower,
kiss of apple,
barbarous bee,
rhythm, rapture, release.

Your skin is a journey
of odor and sound,
of stars
waiting to be born,
sunlight, shade,

and the perpetuation of clarity.
It is youth,
hungry youth,
flood and fire
in a forest of nerves,
savage tongue
that singes the heart.

You breathe on my skin
like you breathe on a fire.

Then the river returns to the pool.

I search for the wounds
of the night's devouring fire,
but find only the warm impression,
a sweet remembrance,
and body perfume.

Awake in the dark

Alone, awake in the dark,
your husband sleeps next to you.
The man who owns your tomorrows,
a proud man, an angry man,
a cold man who'll leave and return
without a word, without a glance.
Cars pass in the distance,
you hear him breathe and you wonder,
you can't remember the color of his eyes.
"They're blue," you say out loud.
You laugh at your voice,
how clear and calm it sounds,
how pretty, you didn't know
you could still be pretty.
Too much yelling, too many tears,
too many wounds that won't heal.
You wonder if anyone told you
how pretty your voice was,
or your hair, or your eyes.
He didn't. You know he didn't
and you begin to hate.
You hate him, hate yourself,
you see how it starts
and how it ends,
how it always ends,
and you begin to cry.
You seek no solace from your tears,
but they are gentle, tender,
they are beautiful and soothe you.

Open heart

The open heart bleeds, like an open heart.

Here it is.

It cannot move through the streets
without seeking the sight of you.

It cannot sit in the sun
without recalling the touch of you.

It cannot beat in the dark
without lamenting the loss of you.

It bleeds. It just bleeds.

Here it is.

Loneliness

I

These are the shadows
climbing the eaves,
the brown light pulling
at the stone street corner.

These are the shadows
and branch at the window,
the red roof tiles
and balcony iron.

These are the shadows
and hills beyond,
the space of solitude
and life sinking through.

II

Loneliness has a clock,
and when the hour arrives,
the weary, monotonous hour,
there is nothing to do,
but wait.

In this hour
nothing lives,
there is only routine,
shadow, fatigue.

III

In love and life,
and lost time in action,
and excess time
in solitude consuming the soul,
life and lovers and people
cry and play
their agonies on the days
until there is nothing.
Nothing but a pressure
that moves one to spin
and toss out words
that speak disorder,
a drive of adrenaline
that strikes and shatters.

IV

If you have never seen
the shadows
on the wall of night,
if you have never heard
the echo of a car,
or a voice,
or a heart
and its steps on the stone,
if you have never known
the silence
of silence,
or if you have known it
for only a time,
and then fled to the warmth
of all that you love
and all that loves you,
if you have never
been truly alone,
you will not know
what is to be learned

in the spirit
condemned to create fire
from its ashes.

V

One would like
to believe many things,
but the only constant
is the progression,
minute to minute,
hour to hour,
lifetime to lifetime.
And mine, ours,
just another novel,
not so finely written,
not so very stirring.
Just pages
that turn like minutes
to hours, to years,
just pages that lead to an end.
And with each death:
destruction,
the annihilation of every tree,
the blackening of every sky,
the end of every universe.

VI

The bubble will break
and darkness will come,
looking for a withered soul
in which to plant roots,

but it won't stay,
one slow bite of an apple
and the light returns:
all is sensation again.

Tonight

Tonight I don't want passion.
I don't want the devouring fire
and its flash of eternity.
Tonight I want peace.
I want the rhythm of your breath
and your breasts against me.

Nothing more.
The day has retired
and taken its sorrows.
We are alone.
We don't have to hide.
For this moment
we don't have to fight
with passion and with tears,
we can rest, be silent,
and let our love grow.

I hold you next to me,
you have always been near.
I hear the clock,
it repeats,
you have always been near.

Dry martini

The drink is silver
entering the soul,
it asks
not to speed the sound,
not to push the pain.

Silver paints walls
of silence in the soul.
It dries and tears,
leaves the marrow
of frightened fingers.

A muffled cry.
A hand on the heart.

Immaculate conception

When he closed the box
it was almost empty.

Hope waited alone.

Feeding on the shadows,
Hope stirred the stillness
and bore Anxiety its child.
The mother and monster embraced,
and from the incestuous bed
sprang the sufferings of the world.

When she opened the box,
it was full, almost empty.

Where the leaves were

The dry snow lines the trees,
gathers and hardens
where the branches meet.
A few leaves remain.

What do you know for me,
you with your skeleton
stretched on the sky?
Is there life after the cold,
after the damp clay dissolving
the spaces where the leaves were,
where the eyes were?
Is it you that rises from the snow,
or do you die with the winter
and your spring belongs to another?

I watch from my window
in the light that reflects us.
You are twisted and silent on the sky.

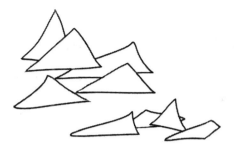

Weep, tears

Weep, crystal tears,
on the marble of my soul.

Carve my breast
from veins of Carrara,
fashion my features
with sharp blows,
and distribute my weight
on strong knees
bent to the ground.

Weep, crystal tears,
on silent stone,
dress me
in dripping light,
and wet me
with white kisses.
Across my eyes
run the tips
of your liquid fingers.

Weep, tears,
spill your silver,
bathe my soul in blue
of whitest stone.

Ocean lesson

You say you want to find
someone who loves the ocean
as much as you do,
loves its waves, its stillness,
and shore.

But I don't know how
you love the ocean,
and I don't know what
you have learned and felt
and become
after years of rising and falling
on your lover's back,
years of riding
the arching sway of the sea.

I can only guess
at the measure and depth,
at the perspective and understanding
born of the union
of individual and expanse,
at the lessons learned
from the loss
and encounter of self.

I can only guess from your eyes
at your romance with sunlight
and moonlight on waves.

I can only guess from your eyes
at the rhythm and pace,
and unrushed abundance
of your heart.

You say you want to find someone
who loves the ocean like you do.
I am willing to learn.
Are you willing to teach?

For Amy

In the middle of a perfect day
of sun and sky and sea,
the surfer waits,
rising and falling
on the swell and sway.

The small splash of kisses
laps at the board,
drowned in the sound
of the intermittent crash.

Patience, acceptance,
she gives herself up
to what the universe brings.
Vigilant, attentive,
prepared to embrace
the sudden ecstasy,
the reconnection
of person and planet,
of offspring and source,
the renunciation of resistance
and wedding
of power, rhythm, and peace.

This is the center
around which her energy revolves,
the connected moment,
the source and channel
of all she has to give.

Later on,
in the rejuvenating relaxation
of exhaustion,
the waves still rocking within her,
she wiggles her toes into the sand
and reconnects
with the solid energy
of the shore.

More loving prints

The beach in the afternoon,
uneven and choppy
with the prints
of playful humans,
humans
of every size, shape, and color,
is the story of a better life.

It is the story of a better way of being,
of treating neighbors,
of mixing lives together
in shared purpose
and common celebration.

The tide rises and falls,
erasing imperfect efforts,
offering a chance to make
more loving prints
in the untried sand of tomorrow.

Siren on the shore

She sits on the shore
staring seaward,
like a siren on the prow of a ship,
longing to feel the salt
splash the stillness of her cheeks
and fill her eyes
with unblinking tears.
The wind reveals its shape
in the dance of her hair.

Her heart carries memories
of stars, storms, and stillness,

guiding and shielding her crew,
embracing the changing shape
of life's voyage
across the curling arms of the sea.

Beyond the surf
the sun slips beneath a cloud
and descends,
casting its last light
in the mirror of her gaze,
and filling her form
with a sudden, blazing fire.

Sunny day

I fell in love with a sunny day,
and was grateful
and accepted
that I couldn't keep it.

I looked for it
day after day
and year after year,
knowing
that each time I found it
it couldn't stay.

It taught me to love
without possessing.

I want to love you
like a sunny day.

Rain on the waves

I sit at my window
and watch the rain fall
on the waves
and on the life and stones
beneath the waves.
The breakers curl,
combing back
the white bangs of the surface,
while the sky soaks
the swelling geography of the sea.

Living creatures and currents
circle above and around
the sunken stones,
while the unfolding force
deposits water dust at the shore.
The rain weeps on the waves
and the seaweed shivers.

Tomorrow I will step into that sea,
leaving behind the waves
of earthly emotions
that rise and fall in my eyes
that gaze through the rain at my window.

The only ones left

"There aren't a lot of us left," said my friend,
referring to our five lifelong friends.

Friends who played board games on rainy spring days,
threw snowballs the first snow,
shot driveway hoops
year after year,
talking of sports heroes, women,
life, and death.

There aren't a lot of us left
that share the same memories
experienced in different ways.

One friend died.
Another couldn't cope
with the monotony of making a living.
Another found joy in contracts and accumulation.

My friend and I are left
to cross paths once or twice a year,
and leap back
to before we knew anything
of real heroes, women, life, and death.

Our futures belong to new faces
creating new memories in our now separate lives.

But our pasts belong to each other,
the only ones left.

Cabin evening

You put a log
in the cast-iron fireplace
and we watch it catch at the edges
and start to burn.

The chimney piping is imperfect
and the room
fills slightly with smoke.

The snow outside is three feet deep
and we lay boards on the surface
to walk to the woodpile.

We talk until
the moon is above the trees.

You put another log in the fire
and we watch it catch at the edges
and start to burn.

Outside a rabbit
bounds through the snow.

In the flickering light
I see you hunt for cups,
and smell coffee
when you open the pouch.

Outside a rabbit
clearly discerns our light.

Staring into the fire

Let me tell you the story
of the fire.

Listen:
the cracking of a whip,
the cries of an abandoned child,
the impassioned moans of a lover.
Listen
to the history of the life of the log,
of its stored energies
released into the arms of the air.

Each story takes its theme
from the nature of the wood.
Here is the story of one
who found the fortune she desired,
and one who regained what was lost.
There is the man or woman in love,
and the man or woman playing tricks
on the man or woman playing tricks.
Each story is its own,
each story is born
of the same fiery source.

And you?
Is your wood slow and deep,
or superficial,
and smoldering at the edges?

Come sit with me,
disrobed,
and feel the heat of the fire
on your naked knees and face.
See the finger of a flame
curl around
the end of the log,
see it lean toward the other flames,

straining to join them,
licking the bark
with glowing tongues.
The pockets of air
pop and whistle,
sending fireworks from the hearth,
and we move back
and lie down,
and let the caressing begin.

Just as the fingers of fire
awaken the wood,
so our fingers and lips
set fire to the skin,
slowly,
starting at the edges,
wrapping and unwrapping,
running the length of a leg,
curling at the calf,
returning to the waist,
climbing to the chest, nipples,
shoulder, and neck,
flashing in a kiss
of wet fire.

No play-act
or pre-meditated passion here,
but two animals
spontaneous and un-reined,
two mammals entwined,
skin to skin and breath to breath,
two lovers
burning yellow, blue, white,
filling the room
with love sound and smell.

Then the bark falls away,
and the glowing heart is exposed,
and the rocking begins.
Wave upon wave
upon wave,
pleasure is reduced
to its elemental state,
assembled and disassembled,
keeping time
to the breathing rhythm,
withdrawing and returning
to the hypnosis
of the undulating glow,
moving through the wood,
turning the once-sturdy log
pumice-light,
a shell in the shadows.

Sit back now,
breathe,
and place another log
on the embers.
The flames rise again,
the mystery is born anew,
and the secret colloquium
resumes its journey
of darkness and light.

Wood burns

The cabin is gone.

The nails and lumber
that were nailed and sawed
by my friend who is gone
are gone.

The nails and lumber
that were nailed and sawed
by my friend who is here
are gone.

My friend who is here
and I
talk about the cabin
that is gone.

The memories that were here
when the cabin was here
are here,
but the cabin is gone.

The memories of my friend who is gone
are here.

The wind that whistled through the trees
before the cabin was built
is here,
but the trees are gone.

Wood burns. People die.

The cabin is gone.
What a fire it must have been!

Eulogy

When he died they said,
"He took time to look at things."

Solitude was the best of him.

It was his key to knowing
and feeling non-human things.

It opened a space for stillness,
and all that was other than him.

Which became him.

He was happy when he was filled
with non-human things.

The sight and sense
of trees and streams and clouds.

The changing hue of intermittent light.

When he died they said,
"He liked to look at things."

Some were glad he did.

Channeling Tu Fu

I

Occasionally,
I free my mind to the day,
I feel the sounds,
the colors, the breeze,
and I remember this day,
which is every day,
a lifetime.

II

The geese fly in formation
from the river to the lake.

My heart follows
while my feet remain on the ground.

The day's last light flickers in the trees,
while the wind sways in the reeds.

I linger in the moving air,
following the flight of the geese.

In the morning my head
will be bowed with responsibility.

III

It rains. The city does not stop.

We have grown beyond the seasons.
We are not deterred by darkness or cold.
We are unfailingly successful.
At what, I don't know.

The business of men and women
is as natural as the sun.

Their movements and delusions
are as clear as a stream.

They criticize what they cannot change,
and embrace what they can.

The ways of men and women
are as natural as the rain.
They vanish like the rain.

IV

Beyond this door ten thousand steps
have sallied here and there
and countless appointments have been kept.

I have remained aloof
but the years have found me.

If my friend were near
we could fill the hours with food and talk.

I have not seen a star in fourteen days.

My sorrow will outlast the night.

V

My friend values my thoughts,
and I value his.

We talk into the night.

The world would not miss us
if we were gone.

VI

The wind that blows along the river,
where did it begin?

What brought it here to find me,
waiting?

The boats on the river
are tethered at the docks.

They rise and fall in independent ways
that belie their independence.
Spontaneity is the product of others.

VII

My friends tell me it's not safe
to walk the streets at night.

They fill me with nightmares
of what might occur.

I know that people perish every day.

But I have crossed swift currents,
and the strength of the stream
made me feel alive.

VIII

The happy donkey grazes in the sun
while the wind blows his ears and tail.

When the wind makes his eyes water,
he blinks and continues to graze.

In the capital the citizens have gone mad.

They are waiting for the first sign of sanity.

In the sun the donkey continues to graze,
and the wind continues to rise.

IX

Before the party is over
I dream of my boat by the river.

It carries me
through damp nights and stream sounds
where stars shine
between canyon walls.
Later,
the stars extend to the grasses.

My boat and my life are tethered
to artificial appliances.

X

The bottle is half-empty.

My friend did not stop by.

He is home, dying.

The faltering light illuminates
the wine meant for him,

and illuminates the empty cup
in my hands.

XI

The grass is green,
the cherry tree blooms,
the robins are fat.

My friend is home from the hospital.

Who knows if this spring
will be his last.

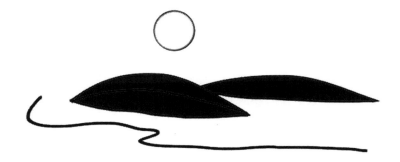

The grass beneath your feet

We sat in the cemetery on lawn chairs,
drinking wine and eating crackers.

It was the first sun of spring
and I sunburned my neck and face.

The next time I saw you
was in the hospital
after your first round of chemo.

What does a man think of
for three months in a sterile room?

Life reduced to breathe-in,
breathe-out, eat only
what you can stomach,
make another slow trip
to the toilet
in order not to soil the bed.

I have seen you jump from
a housetop into a grass yard
and howl with joy.

And I have seen you struggle to speak
with a tube and wire
pushed through your arm to your heart.

There will be fresh grass this spring
beneath bare feet.
The yard, green after so much snow.

You will gaze at the rooftop
and identify the rooftiles that need attention.
They will remain unattended,
while the grass grows thick
beneath your feet.

Dialogue

I miss you.

I have not had a conversation
that flowed freely
from idea to idea
since the last time we sat and spoke.

My life is filled
with justifications,
conversations that demand
a defense of every opinion,
an account of each thought
that slips through the lips.

I miss you,
and the pleasure of spreading
random words in the air,
half-meanings
understood as full meanings,
without debate,
without the wasteland
of so much analysis
that can never create
a connection of the heart.

I miss the sounds,
the silence,
and the understandings
expressed in syllables
shorter than a nod.
I miss eternal truths
declared with smug uncertainty.

My life is filled with specifics.

Dialogues that deconstruct
the pleasure of dialogue.

We will not

We will not fly to Spain again.

We will not break wine glasses, dancing,
at the peak of physical health.

We will not wander streets all night
before early-morning exams.

I will not call at your window
with a pipe and a collection of *Leaves of Grass*.

Our missing friend will not call
at any windows.

But the lights of the city,
seen from the upper Avenues,
will continue to shine and flicker,
and the cars will continue to stream
along Seven-hundred East.

Appreciation

My legs don't work as well
as they used to.

I can't run mindlessly
all day in the park.

I appreciate the steps I take.

I've come to the time
when the joy of appreciation
matches the joy of doing.

At this rate,
I'll be joyful to the end.

As simple can be

The random flakes gather
and accumulate
until the world is
a smooth, unbroken blanket.

And so the random events
of a life unfold,
until all that was uneven,
bursting or sad, is put to bed
in a long, silent sleep.

The random, ragged edges
were as real as real can be,
but the end is as even,
and as simple, as simple can be.

Foreign

Because I forgot
to leave a light on
I had to wait for my eyes to adjust
before I could enter my home.

I had to feel for the lock,
as if breaking in to a foreign door
in a foreign place.

Inside,
I suddenly felt that every place
is a foreign place.

Pieces

The first pieces that don't fit
never fit.

You can try to smooth the edges
and hide them beneath
the parts that do fit.
But the edges poke through
the fabric that separates
security from insecurity.

Unintentionally sharp pieces.
The contours of what we are.

Immutable pieces
that can't be discarded,
without discarding the whole.

Free at last

Things have happened since then.

People have been born
and people have died.

The dead are not afraid
of their neighbors.

They do not see black or white
or any frightening color in between.

The dead are not afraid.

They cannot be swayed
by fearful persuasion.

They are free
to have all they could not have.

Tragedy

The world lives in the future.

The tears you cry now
are tears for the future.
The tears you cry now
are tears cried thinking
of all that was
and won't be again
in the time to come.

Rushing stream of tears,
slow stream of forgetting.

Life reduced
to tearful embrace,
clutching comfort.

Never the same.

No words
for emptiness and fatigue.

The cruelest revelation yet to come,
when the world goes on
as if all that was
never was,
and all that is, remains,
cruel, unaltered, indifferent.

Tragedy.

Life's calendar.

Wind

The day blows the branches,
screaming through the trees.

Cold and empty, the forms
are dull-washed
beneath the colorless grey.
They stand naked
in elemental bleakness.

No swirling snow or rushing rain,
only wind wrapping its arms
round naked trunks and limbs.

Soon the spring will be,
and we know what spring will be,
the ecstatic pain,
the reflex to reach,
the possibility of touch.

But for now, beneath
a motionless layer of clouds,
there is only the wind
that covers and fills
the valley of my life.

Dragonfly

The dragonfly in the yard
is no longer
the precipitous flight
of the river,
but rather
the circling dance of curiosity,
of flight without flight.
The dragonfly lingers,
moving from shadow to light,
while the hornets in the distance
rehearse their grisly dance.

From blade to blade,
which blade
did you choose, and why?
Patch to patch,
light to dark,
just below
my mower's blade.

This day's grass
is tomorrow's detritus.
Don't miss
the bleeding fragrance
of today!

Between infinities

The reflection
of the room
behind me
reflects
in the window
that opens
to the day
before me.

And through
the window
that stretches
before and behind
me,
I gaze forward
and back
from my windowed room.

Then I feel
the soft comfort
of the chair
I sit in,
and I relax
in the security
that a window
is just a window.

Sweet song

You want a sweet song
for your love
that echoes my love,
a song that gives contour
to the borderless light
washing the wall
of a shared room.
You want a song
as sweet as the light
of the moon,
a song like the falling trail
of a falling star,
and the silent pool in the eyes
that catch it.

Well, here it is, my love,
here is your
song and star and pool,
and all the passing promises
that remain
after the last promise
has passed.

Here it is, my love,
the song you were seeking,
take it
and share it
with the rest of your life,
this song I wrote you
for a song,
this sweet song
of forever
that you asked me to sing.

He has an ear

He has an ear
in addition to his ears,
he has an ear.

Hear it hear,
his ear
that has an ear.

He has an eye
that sees
beyond an eye,
an eye
beyond an eye.

He has a voice
that speaks
beyond
what any voice speaks,
a mouth
beyond a mouth.

He has an ear, an eye, and a mouth,
beyond what
he hears, and sees, and speaks.

What every star gazer knows

The message is not found
in the symphony and flicker of light,
but in the spaces between.

Not each light alone,
nor all lights together
can express the music within.

And the words on the page
speak what words speak,
sounding the surface,
while life whirls past
in the spaces between.

Confession

This time I confess.

Without your space
imposing on my space,
I am the cipher
in the unread book.
I am the name
on the unnamed stone.
I am the flower
in the forgotten yard.

Without your space
imposing, intruding,
jarring, and jolting,
I am the empty space
that inhabits
empty space.

Baton

The last flower is gone,
but somewhere its seed remains,
and when the seed is gone,
its flower will remain.

Nothing is whole unto itself.

We are all just vehicles,
and life moves through us.

Auto mobile

The shadows of the mobile
you bought in Venice
navigate on the walls
that meet in the corner.

Wooden fish,
yellow and blue colors,
casting grey shapes
on the walls in the corner.

The flattened shadows
circulate,
passing before and
behind each other,
like faceless people
in faceless streets,
and their passing shadows,
exquisite,
and bereft of color.

Response

We feel obligated to respond
to the question, the call,
or the message
left hours or days before.
The call made at a time when,
for once,
we were engrossed in time,
finally free
of questions, calls, and messages.

We feel pressed,
with so little time,
to respond in an appropriate time,
until finally
we have no time at all,
except for responding
to questions, calls, and messages.

No response

I remember how it felt
to call someone who refused to answer.

Someone who had decided
to live life without me.

Someone who had removed
my image from her earth.

Suddenly the shared planet
became two planets,
one for her, and one for me.

And on the shared planet
which we no longer shared,
I went on half-dead, half-alive.

Missing

What did you miss?

What did you not eat
while you were eating?

What did you not see
while you were seeing?

What did you not touch
while you were touching?

Nothing.

If you were truly
eating, seeing, and touching,
there was no space
for missing.

With persistence

Atrocity is not more prevalent today,
but more transparent.

Bigotry is not on the rise,
but more revealed.

Hatred is no longer ashamed.

The cancer beneath the surface
has exploded on the screen.

It will not be eradicated.

But with chemotherapy,
and persistence,
the organism may yet survive.

I sing the donkey electric

I sing the donkey electric!
A song of asses I sing, near and far!
Asses on hills, asses in fields, asses in herds,
more bountiful than the once-bountiful buffalo,
asses on land and asses at sea, short, skinny, fat and tall!
Multitudes of asses,
spanning these star-spangled states!

I have perceived that to be an ass
is to be enough.

The ears of the ass are sacred, delicate,
twitching receptacles of sound,
assiduous antennae registering, recording all,
the hooves of the ass are no less
than the slippers of sultans
striding silken alfombras and seraglio stone,
the snout of the ass and his nostrils — a dual lamp
of Aladdin — inhaling flowery fragrance,
leading to wished-for fiestas of pumpkin pleasure,
the ass's tail, though stumpy or small, and swatting flies,
is a palm fanning reclining Cleopatra,
his teeth, precious jade, are greened and polished
by the grass of a thousand fields,
his attentive eyes and friendly balance of features,
— courtly countenance and caryatid composure —
no less perfect than the visage of Helen.

Such asses I see, to the north and to the south!
From blistering bivouacs of winter
to blazing battalions of summer,
Patagonia to Peloponnese, Malibu to Manhattan,
Concord to Cambridge, every here
and every there, asses I see! Brown, grey,
yellow, red, purple, orange, azure asses!

Asses in other climes, asses in other times,
French, British, Australian, Arabian, Asian asses!

Eating every blade of grass, an ass!
Trampling every leaf that falls, a hoof!
Wading every stream that sings,
a snout, a snort, and a bray!
Hee-haw goes the jack!
Hee-haw goes the jenny!
Hee-haw go the judge and jury and judged!
Hee-haw from the dell! Hee-haw from the glen!
Hee-haw at mid-day! Hee-haw at the moon!

I see the resigned ass, bearing a load,
obeying the coax of his lord,
I see the boisterous ass braying,
in the barn, his bonny bray,
I see the amorous ass (of these there are many)
expressing exigencies by day and by night,
I see farms, fields, freeways and burgs,
each in their way, replete with asininities,
I see the asinine politician, professor, poet,
each one leaving a brand on the asses of asses.
And the asses of yore, you ask, where are they
with their clip and clop on the stones of the street?
Les ânes voici! I say! Les ânes voici!
Heeding the whinny and neigh,
the ass-bray of the future!

What song do I sing? (you ask and I reply),
I sing the song of asses!
Certain, stoic, and strong!
From each face an ass!
From each office, family, and farm!
Asses I sing! Avalanches of asses!
I sing! I sing a song of asses!
I sing the donkey electric!

Shopping cart dream

He was instantly aware
of the striking differences
of each shopper.
Some jerked him crudely
from aisle to aisle,
pulling his wheels against the grain
and bruising his basket on the displays.
Others steered him
with grace and affection,
gauging the dynamics
of his changing weight,
and he danced with them,
pirouetting through the produce,
gliding past the pasta,
and resting and loading
at the cold beer.

In the bakery section
he would intentionally swerve
to leave a dent
in a loaf of Wonder Bread,
and, spying another shopper,
would brush against
the oncoming cart,
to feel the metallic shiver
rise through his ribs.

Thought

I realize I am just a personal experience
passing through time, but the bathtub faucet
dripping on my toe this evening was real;
as real as anything at any time that has ever been.

Memories

I

Memories,
like smooth stones I can collect
and put in my pocket,
stones I can take out when I want to,
look at, and feel between my fingers.

II

The rusty light of dusk
on wood in autumn,
the damp, fallen leaves,
the simple stream,
and your shadow and my shadow
moving upon the grasses.

You will not lose these.

In the retreating light,
through the cautious mornings
and dampening air,
through the half-lit streets
of memories and dreams,
the light will fall,
and our shadows continue
together within these.

III

The pen needs no ink
to catch the shadows.
It only needs eyes
and ears and fingers
to feel the warmth
on the tips of the leaves.

The silky sprouts squeak
when roots release
their bed by the river.
Green stains on the hands
are enough to remember
the quick fragrance
of the cooling afternoon.

IV

If the moment remains,
it is no flesh and bone,
but photography and gesture.

If the moment remains,
it is the image
in the blood of another.

It somehow returns with the sun.

I go on

What did I see
when I first stepped up
to Paris from the metro at Montmartre?

What moved
in the light among the shadows
in the columns of Saint Peter's?

What whispered
in the mist of Interlaken
when crossing the Brienzersee?

Why the discomfort
and tedious lines that thinned
until I was alone
on a rock shattering the Mediterranean?

Why so many conductors
recording the course of my name?

Why so much motion
when my feet were content to stay slippered
and cuddled on the couch?

An old man crossed
a dirt road
behind a church in Segovia.
His hands and face
were the color of the land,
and his donkey
was laden with stones.
It was clear
he was completely content.

In Paris the sun
woke a drunk asleep
beneath a bridge on the Seine.

He was happy.
He had nowhere to go.

He stopped to ask questions
no one has time to ask.
He took me to meet his friends
fishing on the bank,
and we laughed
and lamented the sadness of change.

From the gypsies in Venice
I expected to hear the same,
but they didn't want to talk.
They offered to read my palm,
and I offered to read theirs.

I wanted to see
how they all fit inside me.
I wanted to see
what my hands had created
with different hopes and dreams.

My past was so heavy
I left it behind and went alone
changing color to fit
the different eyes and places.

I walked and walked and walked,
and did what the natives did.

Then I went to Asia
to find the final pieces
to fit in my mirror.

I stayed in the rain
until my feet grew weary
of foreign floors and uncertain shoes,

and my mouth began to hunger
for the taste of maternal sounds.
Then suddenly I was running,
fleeing from so many people
and places that were not me;
my roots needed water
and could only be nourished
by the spring of my home.

I wonder what I have learned?

Was the answer spelled
in a pattern of bubbles
splashed on a sidewalk in Rome?

Was it whispered
in the song
of a fountain in Seville?

At times a voice will call.
It is an image or an echo
rising from a night in Namur,
lingering on a street in Siena,
or whistling in the wind at Cérbère.

And while I go on here,
a part of me still waits
at an interminable light in Madrid,
or continues in the rain,
stepping through the past
on the stones of Mycenae.

Train ride (France)

Time out of time
on an all-night train.

The sudden jerk and slow pull,
the vague voices ascend
and descend in the distance,
the watchman
walks the platform,
the passing lights flash
on your face and hands,
and the wheels begin to click
to the sway of the car.

You're moving west,
along the coast,
past the silhouette of rocks
and the darkness of the sea,
watching the train lights reflect
on the lurching swell and sway,
on the lines of foam
lifted by the waves
that kiss and shatter.

Then, suddenly,
a tunnel,
you enter the rock,

and the blue lights
spaced along the walls
flash through the window
like the frames of a moving picture,
projecting shadows on the floor.
All the while,
the click and clatter,
the close-surrounded sound,
the echoes from the edges
of the rough-hewn stone.

Just as suddenly,
you emerge
to the unmoving dark,
to the quieting sound,
to the inland shadows
of streetlamps,
a sleeping village,
a car at the light,
the signs, gas-stations,
and the slow-moving shadow
of the rolling train
rising and falling
on the valley and hills.

Darkness
moving in darkness
through darkness,
a succession of time
in a timeless place,
motionless motion,
a hole in the fabric,
a tear in the web,
a moment
infinitely still but moving,
infinitely vast but confined,

a resting planet
roaming through space,
a fixed system
spinning through stars,
a suspended atom
drifting through dark.

All this within
and all this without:

the flashing wave,
the coastal stone,
the sleepy town:

the axis of stillness
racing through time.

Katja (France)

Fresh from sleep she rises,
washes, and braids her hair.
She descends the stairs,
finds a book, and sits to read.

From the bottom step
I look in to see her.
I stay there watching, thinking.

Outside the fog lifts
and the sun breaks through the window.
I feel I am intruding
as I enter the room.

Brushing the loose hair from her cheek,
she looks up, and smiles.

Santiago de Compostela (Spain)

Santiago,
pilgrim paradise,
stone hope and cathedral,
I toast
your cool sun of summer,
I toast
the rosy cheeks of your people
and their breath on the air,
I toast
your alleys and corners
and sloped streets of stone.
You are
the end of the journey,
the flight and release
from flesh-worn fatigue,
you are
the summit of the soul,
the obedient child and generous host,
you are
the reflection
from a winter of rain,
released to an explosion
of green and gold and blue.

Muros (Spain)

Winding down from Santiago,
the estuary was still dry
and the boats
were stranded in the mud.
At the towns children
boarded and descended,
going to and from school.

After lunch my friend and I
walked up over the hill,
out of town,
to see the Atlantic.
From the top of a rock
it spread its blue beneath us,
while the sun extended
its rising reflection,
and the wind whipped our hair.
As the estuary filled,
the fishing boats bobbed
and the speed boats played,
slicing the water.

On the bus ride back,
my friend began a conversation
with a schoolteacher across the aisle.

Cangas de Onís (Spain)

Out of town,
across the Roman bridge,
a dirt road led through a valley
to a group of homes
at the foot of a mountain.
The air was cool and fragrant
with the smell of damp grasses.
Two girls passed and smiled.

On the white-washed wall
of the first home
a sign pointed to a bar.
We entered and four men
looked up in surprise.
A woman at the counter
gave us peanuts and beer,
and commented we couldn't be Spaniards
because we didn't let
the shells fall to the floor.
We smiled and drank slowly,
observing us being observed,
then finished and left with a nod.

Walking back,
the valley in shadows
beneath the sun-tipped hills,
we chatted, and shared a cigar.

Burgos (Spain)

I felt I could live forever,
in Burgos.

Mountain tranquility seeping
down the waters
of the Arlanzón.
Frogs on the mosses,
fishing for flies.
Along the river,
a walkway of canopied green
opening to an old monastery,
empty and abandoned
except for the trees
spreading cotton in the air.
And the clouds,
not billowing on a gust,
but creeping, imperceptibly.

Extremadura (Spain)

At siesta in Cáceres,
I went alone
through the old section,
past the small doors in stone,
past the flowers in the balcony iron,
and beneath the storks chattering
on the tops of church spires.
I walked for over an hour
until I heard voices,
and stopped to see two girls
play scotch with a rope
stretched across a street.

Early next morning,
walking to the station
for the 5:00 a.m. to Madrid,
I passed the gypsies
asleep in the parking
beneath a full moon,
luna llena, luna gitana,
and scraps of a cloud
torn about the sky.

There, on the dresser (Spain)

In the candlelight,
at a little distance,
it looked like something.
A small box, perhaps,
of inlaid wood.

It must have a history,
a history of hands,
a young girl's hopes,
memories, echoes,
and voices from a street.

There, on the dresser,
there, with rich grain and color.
Wood color.

Remember the child's hands, soft and pink,
and as the fingers lengthened gracefully,
clicked with first jewels;
the woman's hands now,
held close to the woman's heart.

Araceli (Spain)

Sitting with straight back
in the soft light from a balcony window,
her clear eyes stared in the mirror.
Her hands drew a brush
through her thick, black hair,
and the slender muscles extended
along the sides of her neck,
as she leaned to pull her hair
back behind one ear.
The pins in her mouth
pressed on her lower lip.
She drew them, one by one,
pinning the locks securely
in a bun at the back of her head.
Carefully, she set the yellow comb.

At the competition
her hands were nervous,
her slender fingers
pulled at one another,
and she bit her lower lip.
A table was set for the judges,
and her mother tried to distract her,
adjusting the pins
and tending to her younger brother.
When she took her place on the floor,
she set her chin and fixed her eyes,
staring past her partner.

A rasgueado, and the dance began...

"Mírala cara a cara, que es la primera,
y la vas seduciendo a tu manera.
Esa gitana, esa gitana, esa gitana
se conquista bailando por Sevillanas."

At first only the slow rhythm,
the circular sway of hips,
then her hands opened like wings,
combing the air, releasing a spell
that hypnotized the public.
Then the continued rhythm,
the sway, the stamp of heel,
and the sudden snap of head.

A pause in the song
set her partner pacing around her,
and when he was done stalking,
the rasgueado started them again...

"Mírala cara a cara, que es la segunda,
cógela por el talle, las caras juntas.
Esa gitana, esa gitana, esa gitana
se conquista bailando por Sevillanas."

Her hands swept her skirt,
her dark eyes flashed,
and her head snapped again.
Another snap, and a pin flew to the floor.
Another, and more pins pulled out,
another, and a lock of hair loosened
and brushed over an ear...

"Mírala cara a cara, que es la tercera,
y verás con que gracia te zapatea.
Esa gitana, esa gitana, esa gitana
se conquista bailando por Sevillanas."

Her eyes flashed again,
and another lock shook loose,
sweeping her neck
and covering one eye.

Still the graceful hands,
the rhythm and sway,
and the motion pulling the pins….

"Es la cuarta, los lances definitivos,
que se sienta en su vuelo pájaro herido.
Esa gitana, esa gitana, esa gitana
se conquista bailando por Sevillanas."

Another snap
and the yellow comb fell,
pulling her hair completely loose.
A turn, a sweep,
a final turn and snap,
and a heel came down
to shatter the plastic crown.

In the ensuing applause
her brother scrambled to gather the pins,
while she rushed, hair streaming,
to embrace her mother.

Photograph (Spain)

Young lady counting coins,
and what is her form later that afternoon?
What tiles sing the stride of her steps?
What cheek knows her touch, what other hands?

And those coins,
what pockets have they found
after their timeless moment in the sun?
And that wood, that iron, those leather straps?

Her shadow,
what walls cast it up to her?
What benches support her weight?
What wrinkles now cover her hands?

Somewhere
the same thought moves the same coins
in small stacks on the same table,
but the soft hands tremble now, they scratch
and are moved from the arms,
like branches dangling in the stream.

Abuela (Spain)

Grandmother,
great grandmother,
sits as a chair sits,
moves as a chair moves.
Her body sleeps,
tucked away,
piled on the stoop.

The laundry leans
on the breeze,
hung out on balconies
and roof tops.
The children play,
popping and squealing,
ducking between the
the colored squares,
they run to grandma,
racing, out of breath,
and flop into her lap.

At Assisi (Italy)

On a clear Umbrian day
we descended from the train
and boarded a bus
for the short ride to Assisi.
A group of visiting monks
chattered their excitement
as we ascended to the stone city.

Off the bus we started climbing,
and on one street I looked
through a small stone arch,
down a short flight of stairs,
and saw a young woman
crouched to feed some pigeons.

We ate ice-cream
and continued to the top,
where we looked down
on the monastery walls
and the scattered rooftops.
In the valley we saw
a train approaching the station.

Walking back we stopped
at a small fountain
and sat in the sun at a café.
We ordered pizza and wine
and didn't worry about the future.

Santuario della Nostra Signora (Verona)

Then they arrived.

Two busloads of children
on a field trip
from a local school
came running
with ice-cream in hand
to the patio that surveyed the city.
Their cheerful teacher
entreated them
to respect the silence,
but the dark heads rushed about,
chasing and gathering
to look out across the river.
They were too short
to tilt the viewing-scope
and saw only the sky,
so one girl lifted another,
peering anxiously into the glass,
letting her ice-cream melt
into her friend's hair below.
The teacher called
and they went off running,
laughing and skipping with the wind.

In the sudden silence,
I noticed the sun
burst through in patches,
and shuffling behind me,
a nun, noticeably shaken.

Foreign lands (Italy)

Foreign lands are real
and remember
blossoms before the bloom,
flowers after the fall.

They remember the fragrance,
without a voice to name it,
that wavers over waters
beyond voices exchanging names.

Perugia (Italy)

I remember at evening in Perugia,
the people walk back and forth
at the promenade atop the city.
After a while you recognize the faces,
passing the restaurants and shops,
and some of them smile.

At one end my brother and I
sat on the stone steps.
We warmed our hands with our breath,
and tried to imagine
being raised on those streets.

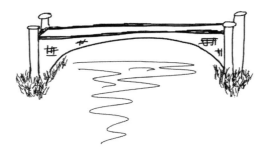

Debora (Italy)

On the grass at Pisa
I met Debora and her friend
studying English.
The breeze blew her hair
and the sun showed her eyes
through her rose glasses.
She had a funny walk
and liked to call me "stronzo,"
showing me the sights
and chattering her contagious Italian.

When she invited me home
I met her mother.
We dined for hours
as the wine softened her eyes,
and she laughed
between quips and compliments.

When I returned for the festival,
watching the candles adrift on the Arno,
she told me how her father died,
and I saw her cry.

In Verona (Italy)

At seven in the morning
I was stirred by the sound
of clinking silverware,
and went downstairs to see.

It was the daughter
of the owner of the hotel,
setting up for breakfast,
spreading tablecloths and arranging
cups, saucers, and spoons.

I could tell she had been doing it
for many years past,
and would be doing it
for many years to come.

It occurred to me,
as I watched her work,
that wherever I might go
and whatever I might do,
she would be here,
preparing these same tables
in this same way.

When she disappeared into the kitchen,
I suddenly felt
that the foreign world around me
was much less foreign.

Before a border (Taiwan)

It takes time
to adjust to the light.
Light not light
but subtle tone and shadow.
Shadow not shadow
but graded light
before a border of darkness.

It takes less-western eyes.
It takes a slow forgetting
of flashing color and screen
and waxed paint on sun-stroked metal.

Wood will help to begin.
Embroidered cushions on floor
and knees beneath knee-high table.
Discordant hypnosis of sounds.
Ritual warming of tea.
Soft skin glow, line and bone.

Fruit stand (Taiwan)

When my new roommate
gave me directions,
he told me to turn down the alley
at the fruit stand.
For ten months I turned there.

The young woman smiled
when I first stopped in.
I had to pick the fruit myself
and let her count the change
from my open hand.
When I learned the numbers,
I pointed, and counted correctly.

The day before I left
she appeared in a new red dress,
hair brushed and pinned,
and I had the words
to tell her she looked lovely,
but somehow,
I didn't use them.

New keys and a trim (Taiwan)

I remember in Taipei,
in one more back alley,
an enormous wooden key
and barber pole.

The first day I sat in the mirror
to watch the woman's hands trim my hair,
there was sun outside,
and the sounds of people and carts
flashed colors through the open door.

After the initial cut,
there was the shampoo massage,
the warm water rinse,
and steaming face towel.
Then more combing, drying,
a final trim and shave,
and the customary cigarette.

I remember when I returned,
steam rising from the breaths
and open pots in the rain,
and ducking into the shop,
after the broken language exchange,
the sound of the blade again,
scraping the hairs
from behind the back of my ear.

Dog (Taiwan)

Individual perception
imparts existence.

Every morning and evening,
coming through the back
where two alleys meet,
was a little black dog.

He always stood there,
motionless in the sun,
and motionless in the rain.
His eyes were swollen,
pink and grey,
and his matted hair exposed
where his skin had broken.

Returning from work,
or returning from a party,
or after two months
when I returned from Spain,
he was there.

I never saw him eat.
I never saw him sleep.

As I passed,
I think he looked at me.

Taipei rain

Pour a little liquor
to wash the mind away.

City lights flashing
on rain-soaked streets.
Stream of lights
and engines
and horns,
noise and soot
in the Taipei rain.
No life in the stare,
in the insanity
of another Volvo,
another necklace,
another stack of cars
stopped and spitting smoke
in the Taipei rain.
Three week rain.

Wash the mind away.

Michelle (Taiwan)

I remember Michelle,
in the soft light
of neighboring apartments
that shone through the window.

I remember Michelle,
sitting on the bed,
her long, dark hair
lying on her bare back,
and the irregular, involuntary sobs
that shook her shoulders.

I remember knowing,
I had never loved more,
and Michelle crying, knowing
my heart was closed.

Narita (Japan)

In Narita, Japan,
on a one-day layover in Tokyo,
I walked up the new sidewalks,
along the new streets,
and past the new homes
to an empty dirt park at the foot
of a hill covered with pines.

The sun was chilly
and dry in the January day.
I napped on a bench,
then walked in aimless circles.
I noticed markings in the sand,
carefully made by children.
In one corner,
a collection of clustering stars,
in another, an enormous sun,
and circling round and round
were orbits and rings,
where the children had shuffled
in starry paths.

From the park I could see
the four-lane to the airport,
and in the distance,
the planes rise above the pines.

Traveling (Mexico)

Water drops,
drop,
drop,
time,
passing slowly,
time to be saved
for another time,
like a book
I can pull from the shelf,
a book of memories,
that for now
I have to keep writing.

Hello (Mexico)

This "I am"
that I am,
is nothing to you.
These eyes and hands
and this face are nothing
but a cracked window
you looked through
on an old bus crossing the country.

These eyes
and face and hands
you looked past.
You didn't see the silver rain
losing its life on the glass.

María Elena (Mexico)

I remember, in Guanajuato,
a young woman
stopped me on the street.
Her hair was back
in a single braid.
One of her teeth
was not straight,
and marked her beauty.

At the garden
we laughed and joked.
I remember she leaned
to write her address
on a paper against her knee,
and I admired the fine hair
on the back of her neck.

Writing, her blouse
pulled forward and exposed
the slim sides of her waist,
and the soft lines that ran
along the sides of her spine.
When she leaned back,
her laughter exposed her navel.

I also remember
when she walked away,
how the sun silhouetted her legs
and hips through her cotton pants.

Ocean gift (Mexico)

From the edge of the bay
I leave you the silence
of a wave after it has broken,
and before the next one breaks.

Traces (Mexico)

Like my brothers, I have found time
to escape time and its burden.
I have found pleasure in distraction,
and satisfaction in its pleasure.

The fugitive light leaves a temporary trace.

One sits, another dances,
still another builds walls of silver
which another with silver shall destroy.

I walk beside the waters,
an insignificant syllable dissolving on the shore.

At Vallarta (Mexico)

At dusk, at Vallarta,
a fisherman casts his net to the sea.

On the rocks his wife waits
as he wades into the waters.

Drawing his net from the waves,
untangling the weights,
he pulls no fish from the webbing.

Footprints (Puerto Rico)

Twilight,
the ocean spray
forms a cool crust
on the white beach,
my feet push through
to the warm sand beneath.
The sand, the spray,
the sound of the waves,
I walk alone.

I have been following footsteps,
small footprints like flowers
pressed between the pages
of a book of memories.
The prints played with the tide,
uneven, irregular,
they dipped near the water
then hurried up the shore.
I imagined you with
cuffs rolled and hair tied back,
the warm waves washing your ankles,
and after only a few steps,
I believed I knew you
and decided to follow.

You didn't seem to mind
that I walk with you,
that I take your hand
and close my eyes.
You opened your arms
to the dreams I brought,
a poetry of wind and waves,
a kiss of spray and song,
a star of shells and foam,
gifts of light from the ocean.

I was about to tell you
how I felt,
when the footprints ended.
I stood a long time
at the edge of the last print,
a print of time, the past,
the last step we would share.
Dropping my chin to my chest
a tear fell,
but before it could land
in your silent print,
it was drowned in a wave,
a wave of tears,
washing your memory away.

Looking up
at the empty beach ahead,
the sun now completely covered,
I took a breath
and continued, alone.

Moment's fire (Puerto Rico)

From dark roots entangled
will rise a moment's fire,
a reckless, uncautioned candle,
whipped by the breeze in the clouds.

The spark grows wild in the wind.
The eyes flash from the fire.
Then the flower returns to the root.

The eyes die (Puerto Rico)

The eyes die
and the head is heavy,
the dark weight of gravity
pulls me to the ground,
it is difficult to breathe.
Life is reduced, it flees,
gives way to a fixed, blank stare.

Each face is a challenge
I cannot meet. Fear,
fear you are watched,
laughed at, rejected.
The world takes me,
I have no strength to resist.
Throw me here, throw me there,
I walk vacantly,
I close my eyes and walk,
until the day is through.

Happiness (Puerto Rico)

I pull back the covers,
sit and take both feet off the floor,
and slide them
softly between the sheets.

Deep breath, Mmmmmm.
Sigh, smile, sigh.
The world is happy tonight.

Words hide and seek in the dictionary,
socks play tag in the drawer,
the fan is dizzy with love,
and molecules line up one by one
for a gentle ride around the room.
Woof, woof, woof, a dog barks. Another.
And pillows relax in the corner.

Chennai (India)

When the flight descended
to Chennai
I was astonished
by the lack of city lights.

On the way to town
the figures on the side of the road
were black silhouettes in the dusty night.

Desperation had brought me there.

The broken cement of the sidewalks,
the fluorescent shop lights,
the reused-plastic bottles of water.

The first night was a sea of shadows.

In my hotel room the small cockroaches
fled when I turned on the light.
The large ones were found later,
dead by the shower drain,
after the maid cleaned the room.

Every dark face I engaged, engaged me.

The ones I didn't engage
moved past like currents in a stream,
and I was one more current.

Moving from eyes to current,
I went from everything to nothing.

I remember a little girl
sitting alone on the sidewalk,
making shapes with bottlecaps,
while the traffic and steps of a thousand feet
clamored around her.

Understanding (India)

They are so poor,
you can never understand.

They are so poor
they could sit with you,
talk with you,
hold your hand
and caress your cheek
with their broken skin,
and you would only see
skin, cheek, and hand.

You might imagine
you see within.

You might imagine
you know the noble blood
fighting the bite of fire,
and you might steal the light
of so much suffering,
to take home and cuddle
in self-contented pride.

You might imagine
you feel with a special
perceptive compassion.

But no.

They are so poor,
you can never understand.

Gaelic morning

The swollen lichen and grasses
soak the leather of my shoes,
and my laces click
to each step I take.
The sky is a line of grey
above the growing green
and black rock
of the mouth of the sea.
The wind wanes for a moment
and doesn't penetrate
the crochet of my sweater.

I'm walking on blood-rich soil,
filled with fallen ancestors,
men, women, children,
with requisite hopes and worries,
joy and sorrow,
and copied musculature striding
these same rocks and grasses.

And all the while
the same struggle for palace power,
and the same limits of patience,
perseverance, and personal integrity,
invisible limits revealed in an instant,
that, when crossed,
welcome the onrushing fight,
to the death, for limits,
the noble fight,
for the soul of this land
robbed of its soul.

The war cry
and death wailings

are unheard today
in the grey-closed morning.
But the village voices
and laughter of children,
still sing
in the click of laces
and swish of grass
about the ankles.

Gaelic evening

The full moon is scarcely visible
behind the cover of clouds:
a dissipated yellow-brown glow,
spreading dispersed particles
of misty light.

The world is damp and chilled
beyond the warmth
of my woolen coat.

The sea repeats
its frothy sound,
surprised by the sudden resistance
of stony shore.

In the distance
the village lights reveal
the underside of the clouds.

My cheeks are cold
and my eyes are bright
beneath my woolen cap.

Gaelic rain

With the grey slap of thunder
the rain begins,
and the blanket of the sky
covers the town with its staccato sound.

The tongues of vegetation
drip with cold refreshment,
and the earthen path
grows muddy on the feet.

Silver street
and damp building stone,
splash of wheels
and distant rumble,
the rain falls on garden gates
and roof spines,
while inside,
the evening fires begin to burn.

Albuquerque sun

At seven years old
I used to swing at sunset
and sing to the extending shadows.

A certain sunshine on the roofs,
on the portable pool,
a certain sunshine when setting out
the luminarias for Christmas,
a certain sunshine and dust
at the fence by the alley,
a certain sunshine,
vines and sand and trees,
by the clothesline in the yard.

That same shine today,
stirring memories,
like particles of dust in the air.

Preston, Idaho

I look back on Preston,
I return there
and want to return there
and the loving is gone.
The street signs are rusted
and the streets are broken.

Only the fields remain,
the new flowers,
the rising wind
on seas of grain,
the green towers
and labyrinths of corn.

This is the Preston I preserve,
the house at the end of the road,
the ditch and wire and tree,
the rain on the windows.

I took the small stuffed animals
from grandma's cabinet before the funeral.
I remember upon stepping outside,
the chilly breath and rush of air.
My feet left dark traces
on the silver grass,
and my voice on the grey sky
left silver sounds.

My mother's eyes

My mother's eyes, looking
upon the smiling child,
the child
that looks now upon her,
her memory, her image,
her flesh gone. Her dream alive.

Do you know
what life and death mean
among the gardens?
Can you see
the eternal empty spaces?

You see,
my mother came smiling
upon this world,
smiled in turn
on her children,
then died slowly,
eternally,
against her will.

Steven Snow

Torn clouds at dusk glowing
behind the skeleton of a tree.
Right-angle of well-constructed home,
feel of wood braced by sturdy fingers,
transformation of form into structure,
and the continuation of nature through Steve.

All things that entered his eyes
entered his body, heart, and soul.
Nails, screws, boards, stumps, seeds, sprouts,
loam of earth on shoes left outside the door.
All things revolved in his center,
mixed, melded, transformed
by a merry love of shapes,
shapes to sit on, look out of, make music with,
primal shapes making primal sounds,
wordless, accessible, joyous shapes,
emerging from transforming hands.

The nuts, bolts, and lumber
of my youth passed through his hands.
Laughter, love, and friendship
were held in his hands.

Master and slave to substance,
son of the didgeridoo and drum,
loving, catching, releasing,
hunting beauty in the mistake,
in the controlled accident
of ink on hide, of grain in wood.
I offer these words to you, Steven Snow,
beast of burden with a poet's soul,
I offer these words to remember you,
hoisting and bearing
stones to the top of the hill,
then rejoicing at the prospect
of the shared walk back down.

Clair

Every time I see snow
I think of you.

You know more
about the variations of snow
than I know
about words on a page.

Gravity, texture, rhythm.

You play with mountains
like the sea plays with waves.

Balance, vulnerability, control.

When you come to the edge of a cliff,
I'm sure you want to throw yourself
into the widening expanse.

Hilarie

A single obsession of light,
a single smile
in the soil of the soul,
a flash in the shadow,
a burning planet,
a single note from the spheres.

A single light illuminating
the water's crash
at the cliffs of the heart,
a leaping light of statues
erected and razed in the foam,
an undulating light reflecting
the swell and hollow and sway.

A simple light persisting,
in absence,
an extinguished star that continues.

Your eyes

The shades of sky
in the seasons
are not so numerous
as the shades of your eyes.

With dawn's first glow
they opened,
extracting light
and drinking color,
singing
with the play and splash
of the stream.
Hills, feathers, and branches
were the instruments
of their song,
and they went reading
the notes of the day,
reading its words,
(reading these words),
and casting their image
in the reflecting eyes
of another.
They continued,
sharing their illuminated
give and take,
until twilight
released its rivers
and your eyes,
like the tip of an alpine peak,
caught the last sparks
of fleeting fire.

Through electric shadows
they carried their light,
until evening closed
and they opened anew,
stars,
in the night of your dreams.

Moonrise

Just outside whirl the sparks
and the planets in space.
Their silver tails leave wounds
on the dark glass of the sky.

Tonight the moon mounts
the slow steps of the spheres,
raised like an idol by holy hands,
scaling the edge of the night.
At the summit the light lingers,
awaiting its worldly worship,
then descends again, riding on ropes
borne on the back of the air.

Like a white pyramid,
or a burning crystal,
the heavens have been set for you.
They light and carry your name
to a place beyond the sound
of the whistle and whirl of stars.

The moon found you

Caught in the discarded sheets
at the foot of the bed,
the broken rays reached toward you.
Like timid fingers they touched lightly,
then relaxed, embracing your ankles.

Slowly, like a child entering water,
you were immersed in the light.
It moved like a gentle river
illuminating your cool flesh,
then flowed to the circles of your knees
and grew in two rich currents
to meet at the top of your thighs.
Pausing, rising and falling with your breath,
the tender waves rolled to your neck,
caressing your arms and breasts.

As the light reached your eyes
I feared it might wake you,
so I blocked it with my hand
and let you go on sleeping.

With two hands

With two hands and a full heart
I have fashioned a poem.

It was born of a fragrant branch
cut from the top of a white mountain.
With delicate blade I shaped it,
refined its roughness.
I smoothed, sanded, and stroked it
until it had the softness of your skin.
With a dark varnish
I released the blood in its veins.

It was born as you were, it is yours.

I traveled the winds of salt,
where the waves ache
and the rivers meet and mix.
At a silver lake I listened.
I crossed the seasons
and found in the fountains of spring
the voice that knows your name.

With earth on my hands,
I bring this poem
to the silent place where you keep
the secrets of your heart.

I cannot offer

The hills do not know me
and the waves erase my name.
I cannot offer the gifts of the earth.

I cannot offer the broad mountain and wild rose,
the moody sky and its quarreling clouds.
My feet are frightened,
they fall on the rocky path,
and they tear on the virgin thorns.
Because its rivers do not call me,
I cannot offer the gifts of the earth.

But you sprang from the soil.

You awoke in the blue day
that echoed in the trees,
opened your arms, and embraced the dawn.
Your voice flew from branch to branch,
and your happy feet played,
laughing with the stream.
The wind whispered secrets of the stone,
and the sun sketched your soul
with stretching shadows.

I cannot offer the earth,
so I wait the night in silence
to admire your midnight crown.

The night

Come, the day has been waiting,
like a boat in the rain.
It opens now, behind the branches,
pulling its clouds
past the moon on the fjord.

Down to the dock
I will follow the stars
and the sound of your steps
on the needles and twigs.

With my gaze to the light,
I will row to the moon
on the silver sparks' splash
in the sky of your eyes.

At the island the boat
will knock and bob,
and my open hand will offer
the night that will never return.

Poem of assurance

Be not alarmed
by the nightingale's song,
by the sudden moon
that seeks to praise,
fear not the night's serenade
pulled from the strings
of an honest heart.

The age rings fear
in society's suspicious eyes,
yet the bird still attends
its suitor's song,
the flower still savors
the sun's delicious buzz,
and the grass drinks deeply
the silver kiss of dawn.

Be not alarmed
by twilight's liquid tones,
rather relish its leaves
singing at your window,
so that evening's anxious room
will echo sweet melody
when night curls itself to sleep.

A lesson in beauty

Because the flowers hide patiently
under the cool blanket of autumn,

because the spring comes quietly
with the sound of melting snow,

because the breeze touches softly
with the fresh fragrance of summer,

I will have to learn to see, to listen
and to feel, if I am to find you.

Too many words

Oh lady!
Too many words
and too much motion
to describe the branch's sway
and the afternoon of your eyes!

Buzz, hum, and flutter are slower words.
City whisper heard from the hills,
and voices' splash crossing the canyon.

Seep in, stillness,
settle the swell of the sea!

Too many words
and too much motion
to feel the feel of the earth,
the grass beneath the feet,
the water's spray upon the cheek.

With so little wisdom,
with circles and struggles and haste,
how can I hope to catch the ripple
of your breath on the glass of my soul?

Fortune

A drop of rain that falls
is more fortunate than I.

Your pack and your books,
your clothes and hangers and shoes,
the cups in your kitchen,
the spoons in your drawer,
the pencil and page
and every thing you touch,
is far more fortunate than I.

The grass beneath your heel
is more fortunate than I.

What you hear, what hears you,
is much more fortunate than I.
The bird at your window,
the walls of your room,
the pillow that catches
your whispering breath.

Everything that sees you,
the sun breaking through,
the passing stranger,
the dogs and cats,
and the drowsy driver
waiting at the light,
are far more fortunate than I.

Your mirror is infinitely fortunate.

A drunk on the stoop
squints to see you pass,
and is far more fortunate than I.

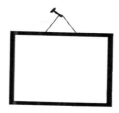

In an instant

Easily,
in an instant,
you could have not been born.

You could have had nothing.

You could have lost
the sun, the sky,
the slow moon ascending,
and the harmony
and flicker of leaves.

You could have lost
the rain's splash
exciting the soil,
the blue beyond,
and the light
and absence of light.

You could have lost everything.

And I could have lost the same,
never knowing the cure
for thirst in a world without you.

Echo

Narcissus leans
over the crystal stream,
while Echo,
restricted to repetition,
waits for the words, "I love you."

This is a mirror of sound.

As Echo waits for Narcissus
to speak what she longs to repeat,
so these words await your lips
to pronounce the same to you.

Room for two

Tonight in the rain,
there is room enough for two.

Tonight at the window,
our breaths would meet and mingle.

My eyes look out across the city.
Where are you beneath
the flash and laugh of the lights?

Retreating from the window,
the rain would guard the warmth,
and meeting of lips and mouth.

It is early

Of course, it is early.
You will hear other voices
sing other songs.

You will choose one.

You will come to know
the depth of the shadows
in the grasses.
You will see friends
grow and wither,
and dreams and sorrows slip away.

Will you forget these songs?

Will they vanish in the beauty
with which they cannot compete,
the white mountain, the red rose,
the resolute eyes of a lover?

Or will they remain,
and remind you of the glow
your eyes had once,
and the magic they inspired
in the heart of another?

Your bike

From slow hills
I turned a corner
and suddenly before my eyes,
a singing star,
a white arrow,
a silver leap and splash
in the stream,
a sudden kiss
that could only be you,
riding the ray of your bike.

Down the hill
you darted and dived,
maneuvering through
fatter fish,
sailing the stones and tongues
of white water,
slowing,
drifting,
circling in an eddy,
curling at the 4-way,
then pushing again
to the arms of the stream,
sailing its light
to the mountain and lake
of your home.

Turning again,
I was too late to follow,
and found only the sound
buzzing on the water,
like the silver-blue wings
of the dragonfly.

Of the earth

Oh love, if not for you
the seasons would surely die!
Of all things human
you alone belong to the earth.

The dark soil breathed
and the grasses sang
until they were strangled
with slow cement.
To construct their shelters
the people went to the hills,
where they razed
the orchestra of the trees,
stripping their strings,
so the limbless trunks
could be stacked and sold,
and only silence remained
where the music had been.

Not satisfied with a single roof,
they hired bandits
to return with their blades,
seeking the slow heart
of the sequoia,
while the politicians at their windows,
unable to see through the smog,
signed with white hands
the death warrants of the hills.
The rest
sat stupidly in their homes
watching the walls grow,
until there was no door
for day to enter,

no crack for the wind,
and the dim light remaining
was tinted and conditioned.

When their prisons were complete
they thrust their hands
beneath the soil,
and melted its singing metal
into the graceless lines
of their cars.
In the sudden haste
they went from house to house,
smelling of synthetics,
stepping out only long enough
to curse the wind's breath
disheveling their hair.
They put wheels on their homes
and carried them
groaning up the canyon.
They spread like a plague
through the trees,
splashing the branches
with obscene shapes and colors,
until dust rose
where the flowers had been,
until engines roared
where there had been birds,
until the water ran black
where there had been light.
They left their broken trail
of plastics and noise
until even the wind could not wash
their memory from the trees.

Oh love, if not for you
the seasons would surely die!
Of all things human,
you alone belong to the earth.

Your white feet
stepped from the foam
like polished shells
washed upon the shore,
and bending with the curl of the waves,
your slow breath copied
its repeated rhythm and sway.
You played with the tide,
dipping near the foam,
and the jealous sea reached
to pull you back,
but its frothy fingers
touched only your heels,
then stretched
and expired in the sand.

Your feet continued
across the hills and fields,
moving in perfect balance
when the earth narrowed to a log
fallen across the stream.
They continued
past the toppled remains
of the beaver's winter work,
and along the unscarred path
of the deer's narrow trail
that led back
to the bank of the singing brook.

It was there your eyes learned
their color from the branches
and stole the silver light
of the stone's push upon the stream.

It was there your hands learned
the circling chase of the birds,
and your hair stole its aroma
from the cool in the shadows.

It was there your heart learned
the wisdom of the water.

Oh love, if not for you
the seasons would surely die!
Of all things human,
you alone belong to the earth.

When the wind whispered your name
you followed it to the top
of a red-rock mountain.
It pressed its kiss against you,
running the line of your chin and cheek,
and caressing with delicate patience
the curve and lilt of your ears.
There, braced against the wind,
the extending light
caught and filled your form
with its rising breath of fire.

Kristi

They were introduced at a party,
just as he was coming in
and she was going out,
and he noted that she was cute,
not tall, and slender
in her fleece Patagonia coat.
Her jeans were relaxed
on her legs and hips,
her loafers looked comfortable,
and her curly brown hair
was full on her shoulders.

Two months later they were sharing
a pot of tea for their first date,
and she spoke of teaching children.

It was early Spring and they
decided to walk around a park,
but she received a text message
from her daughter and apologized
that she had to leave early.

On the way to their cars
she found a large nail discarded
in the dirt by the sidewalk
and presented it to him as a memento
to preserve the moment.
She agreed to meet him later
that evening at his home.

The major pieces of the picture
were all in place.

Home

She lives in an air of gratitude,
feeling she is not deserving
of the gifts that gather in her home.

Home is where her heart is,
and her heart is her home.

Her quest is to carry inside her
a feeling of home,
the home she left behind
when she was the youngest to leave,
the home she takes with her
wherever she goes.

A single stop-light and grocery,
dueling drug stores,
and summers driving a tractor
on her grandfather's ranch.
She stared through the windshield
of his pickup at the cattle,
and the insects, illuminated
in the dying light.

She carries that light inside her,
and that light is her feeling of home.

Are you the latest person to be near her?
Welcome home.

Holding hands

She had pictures of all
her family and extended family
on the fireplace mantel
and in the cabinets on either side.

He had heard their stories
and remembered what he could,
but he had only met them in passing
at her daughter's wedding.

He only met her friends
when they happened to stop by.

Because they worked at the same college
and she didn't want her colleagues to know,
he rarely went with her
when she went to socialize,
and they didn't hold hands in public,
because someone might see and talk.

The restrictions inhibited the roots
that were growing together.

At night he dreamed
of holding her hand on the street.

Living novel

He saw all the pictures of her
and her family
waterskiing on the lake.

And the prom-queen photos
she was embarrassed to show.

And he heard the stories
of the home discipline
that set the spark
to her rebellious spirit.

He thought of writing a novel
with the stories from her town.

But he realized it would be superfluous,
when he could hold the living novel
right there in his arms.

Walden Pond

Half-way around the pond
they met a man
fishing on his lunch break.

The only other visitor
was paddling a kayak
along the opposite shore.

At sunset they strolled
the Shady Hollow Cemetery,
and the next morning,
on the way to the station,
she got a message
that her father had died.

On the station bench,
holding her in his arms,
he wished her pain was his pain,
and her tears his tears,
so he wouldn't have to see her cry.

The ash grove

Her life revolved around a single song.

Down yonder green valley, where streamlets meander,
when twilight is fading, I pensively rove.
Or at the bright noontide, in solitude wander
amid the dark shades of the lonely ash grove.

'Twas there while the blackbird was joyfully singing,
I first met my true love, the joy of my heart.
Around us for gladness the bluebells were ringing,
ah! then little thought I how soon we should part.

She and her siblings sang it with their father as children.

Still glows the bright sunlight o'er valley and mountain,
still warbles the blackbird his notes from the tree.
Still trembles the moonbeam on streamlet and fountain,
but what are the beauties of nature to me?

With sorrow, deep sorrow, my bosom is laden,
all day I go mourning the one that I love.
Oh! gentle leaves tell me, where is she waiting?
"She's sleeping 'neath the green turf down by the ash grove."

And sang it again at his funeral.

The ash grove how graceful, how plainly 'tis speaking,
the harp wind through its branches has language for me.
Whenever the light through its branches is breaking,
a host of kind faces is gazing on me.

The friends from my childhood again stand before me,
each step wakes a memory as freely I roam.
With soft whispers laden its leaves rustle o'er me,
the ash grove, the ash grove, again is my home.

It was the story of the seasons.

My lips smile no more, my heart loses its gladness,
no dream of the future my spirit can cheer.
I only can brood on the past and its brightness,
the dear ones I long for again gathered here.

With sorrow, deep sorrow, my bosom is laden,
all day I go mourning for the ones I have loved.
Their voices whisper softly, for me they are waiting,
they're sleeping 'neath the green turf down by the ash grove.

And the continuity of their lives.

Humility

She had too much humility
to ever believe
that he liked what he liked about her
as much as he did.

There were things he didn't like,
but those were reflections
of things he didn't like about himself.

The things he did like,
he liked as much as he had ever liked
about anyone else.

And he told her,
but she had too much humility to hear him,
and never believed
he liked her as much as he did.

Blueberry donut

She scolded him when he bought
a blueberry donut at the neighborhood store.

He didn't want the donut
as much as he wanted to be playful
and see if she'd play along,
but she was focused
on shopping as quickly as possible
in case a colleague was hidden in the aisles.

Back home she let down her guard
and was a willing participant
in games she had never played before.

Beyond words

They both liked analytical argument,
to a point.

When it went beyond his point,
he tried to end it by getting short.

He could sometimes see
what others could not see,
but he was set
in most of his ways.

Dogma was a shortcut
to get to things he liked better,
to get to things beyond dogma:
poetry, touch, and song.

He was often in a hurry
to get to where he could slow down.

He was often in a hurry
to reach the timeless hours of touch.

When he touched her,
he told her over and over with his hands
how he loved her,
but he never used the words.

If he had used the words,
would she have believed them?

Under the covers

They read Mary Oliver in bed
by the light
of the bed-table lamp.

He read slowly
and she listened,
and then she asked him
to read it again.

He did and they talked.

Then they turned out the light and,
under the covers,
he touched her bare arm
with his bare arm.

Lines that connect

Never have two forms
fit more closely together.

As if they had been born
of a single piece,
broken along the lines
of enticing contours,
lines that never tire
of fitting back together,
lines whose excitement
the fingers long to touch,
limbs and hills and valleys,
and forests of nerves
sending lightning
through the blood.

Soft lines, resting,
tossed across
the relaxed lines of the other,
reunited
in the restoring waters of sleep.

Barefoot in the kitchen

Late at night,
after blowing out the candles,
they would drink water
in the dark kitchen
illuminated by
the neighbor's porch light.

The floor tiles were cool
on their bare feet,
and the porch light was white
on their bare skin.

In the morning light

He looked at her in the morning light
and wanted to continue looking,
but she didn't like the way she looked,
although it was clear
he certainly did.

He liked to look at her
as much as he had ever liked
to look at anything.

But she wouldn't believe him,
no matter how long he looked.

The reason for his song

She was the only one
who could spend a day in his arms,
without getting restless.

And she was the only one who could listen
to him play guitar and sing
until he ran out of songs to sing.

She was the reason,
before he ever met her,
that he learned to play and sing,
so that one day
he could play and sing
to someone, the only one,
who could listen
as long as he could sing.

Before he ever met her,
she was the reason for his song.

Two streams

When they sat down together
for the first time in days,
they were like two streams,
flowing one past the other.

They each had stories to tell
and things on their minds,
and even when only one was talking,
the sound of the different streams
fought the sound of listening.

Later, in the evening,
the streams flowed together
in single harmony,
a harmony without words.

Sheep

After an all-night rain they woke
in their van to a campground full of sheep.

The shepherds had been herding them,
and a flank had drifted into the trees
and the empty camping sites.

She immediately ran to be with them,
as the sun slipped through the clouds,
and later, she told him of a dream
to have a house in the country,
with a goat and sheep in the yard.

Frost on the windows

Their breaths frosted
the windows of the van,
sleeping on a road
outside of Lolo Hot Springs.

She was comfortable camping anywhere.
Nothing bothered her.

Sharing her body warmth
beneath the piled-up covers,
he would have been happy
to never get up.

Soul of a poet

She was the one who told him
to publish his poems.

She was the one who gave him
ideas to write.

Ideas born of conversations
argued or agreed upon the day before.

She never knew how many poems
she wrote for him.

He had the words,
but she had the soul of a poet.

Getting out

She was in her head
and he was in his head,
and when he was ready to get out,
she wasn't ready,
and he snapped at her and hurt her,
because she didn't understand
that his head was not
where he wanted to be,
and that he needed to get out
long before she did.

Once he got out,
and stayed out for a while,
he didn't snap at her,
but loved her,
and when she got out,
he loved her like he loved
the stream and leaves and trees,
like the sun shining
through the window of his van,
warming them where they napped
on the bed in the autumn air.

They sat at the table

They sat at the small dining table,
and he wasn't listening.

He was still talking to himself, silently,
about what had upset him
that morning, noon, or afternoon.

And he missed the remedy
she was putting into words,
the remedy, like a jewel,
she was putting in his hands.

154

Predictable

They were both predictable
on certain topics and themes,
and one push of the well-worn button
would send them circling
in their automatic feedback.

It would soon seem pointless,
and the loop would become
an argument for argument's sake,
until the one with the short temper
would lose his temper,
and the one with patience
would regain her composure
and wait for the storm to subside.

Other times they circled
in mutual agreement,
reinforcing familiar convictions.

They were like any two people
spending long hours at the table,
sharing each other's minds.

For a time

He was often like a lumberjack who couldn't hear
the slender voice of the stream.

He was a heedless hiker,
trampling young ferns and flowers.

He was a shout bellowing across the lake
through the unblemished air.

And she was the stream, and flower, and air,
and for a time, she loved him.

The movie

They watched a movie after
the sun went down in the sunroom,
and he moped.

He was angry about something
but he didn't know what.
She didn't know either,
and thought he was angry at her.

In his anger he criticized the film
and she thought he was criticizing her.

She didn't have that kind of anger,
and didn't know there was nothing to do.

When the movie was over,
she got up to heat a glass of water,
and he continued to mope.

Competition

He tried to convince her
of the benefits of competition,
the drive to improve,
and the debt you owe your rival.

He tried to convince her
that screaming and yelling at the screen,
cheering one against the other,
was not harmful to anyone.

But all she could think of
was Libya, Syria, Ukraine,
and defenseless Kurds
being slaughtered,
just because a horde of sign-waving zealots
wanted to crown an American king.

Grandson

She was reborn when he was born.
She was a child and a mother again
the moment she became a grandmother.

And every lesson she had learned
from experience
and a career of learning to teach,
was ready for the new individual,
the individual who taught in an instant
more than she had ever learned.

She worries at night
about the world that awaits him.

And just yesterday she complained
about a baby bear in a story book
whose behavior was far too aggressive.

Nothing profound

She rarely gets a good night's sleep.

Every night she lies in bed, thinking.

Nothing profound, she will say,
just thoughts
of what she can do for others,
thoughts of kindness,
of family and friends,
her grandson,
and all that awaits
the ones that she loves.

Nothing profound, she says,
just love,
and the weight of the world.

Reading

He loved to read to her,
but didn't do it often enough.

More often,
he was lost in thought,
hearing himself think,
gathering sounds, shapes, and colors,
into words,
writing the poem
he had not yet written,
translating the late-afternoon light
into ink on a page.

They had read *Cien años,*
and *Captain Harvey,*
translations of Neruda
and his own original poems,
but there was still *Don Quijote, Vanity Fair,*
and all the Austen, Yeats, Shelley,
and classics he had never read.
But the sad news of the day,
the tragic, death-of-democracy news,
almost always intervened,
and he would find himself
repeating
the same dogmatic opinions
of what should and must be done.

She listened patiently
as he went on repeating,
never knowing about the things
that he wanted them to read.

To write a poem

She pointed out he had never
written her a poem.

She could not be his soulmate
if he had never written her a poem.

He had written sugary collections
for strangers who passed for a moment
and then were gone.

He had not written her a single verse.

What she didn't know was the poems
had all been written in the living.

Putting them on paper was just scribbling.

Scribbling that could only be done in solitude,
the solitude he had, once their bond was broken,
because she could not be his soulmate
if he had never written her a poem.

Soulmate

The word "soulmate"
was the beginning and the end.

He said it when he talked about past illusions,
and she heard it as a criticism of what she wasn't.

He was wrong and she was wrong.

It was neither of those things.

It was standing right in front of them,
but they just couldn't see.

The book

She was surprised when she opened
the gift-wrapped package
and found the book that told the story
of a part of her life.

No one had ever recorded
her life in words before.

She blushed at parts
and cried at others,
just as she had
when she lived those parts.

As she read,
the clock continued its measured march,
carrying her
and everyone else
closer to the final page.
But somehow with the book in her hands
the clock stopped a beat.

Too late

When he finally saw
what he had not seen,
what he had overlooked
when he was blinded
by what he expected to see,
it was too late.

She was gone,
and might never return.

He will miss

He will miss her soft eyes.
He will miss her hair.
He will miss her rough hands
and their grip upon him.

He will miss her firm shoulders,
the perfect proportion
of her naked form,
her surprising passion,
and her ability to let go.

He will miss her fingers
clicking at the keyboard,
typing the lessons she hopes
will make for a better world.

He will miss watching her walk,
moving in easy balance
around the kitchen.

But most of all he will miss
what she still had to teach him,
the things that she is and does
that are lacking to his heart.

He will miss her patience
and forgiveness
for all the times that he wasn't
what he could have been.

Ode to the happiest steps I've climbed

I walk the short, sloped driveway,
up the two cement steps
and the four tiled steps
to your door.

I ring the doorbell.

You pull open the wooden door,
and push open the glass door,
and smile, and invite me in.

Ode to the photographs on the shelves
on each side of your fireplace

The photographs of your family,
framed in little frames,
watch your life
from their place upon the shelves.

They are the reflections
of the different parts of you,
the stories of your life
woven into theirs.
They are stories that lead
to a captured moment in time,
and then go on
to another place and time.

They keep time past from becoming past,
and keep all times present in the present.

You move through your house
like moving through a reunion,
and each photo transports you
to a place beyond your place,
to another path and moment
branching from your center.

Your house, like your heart,
is where the times and places
of your life meet and mingle.

When I step into your home,
I start a journey through your heart.

Ode to your loveseat

Yellow loveseat couch,
against the wall,
looking out
the living-room window,
the window that looks
down the tree-lined street
where neighbors do
their neighborhood things,
you wait for me
to sit in your lap,
or nap
with my head on one of your arms
and my feet on the other.

You are the bed
where my body rests
while I listen to my love
tell tales of family and friends,
or challenge my statements
with insights
and more hopeful points of view.

You are the softness
that supports me
as I gaze at the softness of my love,
curled in her chair,
swaddled in my guitar song,
drifting from attention to sleep.

Other times,
you hold us both in your arms
as we look out on the weather,
on the sun, and the rain, and the snow,
while the hours pass
uncounted,
secure in the shelter
of shared presence.

Ode to your dining table

Small, wooden table,
with four chairs squaring
your roundness,
you spend most of your day
as the desk
where my loved one works,
sending signals into cyberspace.

You are the center of everything,
the nexus that connects
one room to the others,
one person to another,
and each day to the next.
You are the first place
my love sits in the morning,
and the last place
she sits before bed,
and when sleep doesn't come,
you are the pre-dawn companion
who keeps her company
through the night.

On special occasions you expand
to accept additions to your surface
and length to your perimeter,
embracing new visitors
and random chairs.
Upon your back is laid
the bounty of the world,
while above your leaves
shines a shared light,
and a smiling exchange of eyes.

You are simple, and solid,
and ask nothing
but to stand and support,
to carry and offer and serve.

Ode to your refrigerator

A sea of snapshots,
a smorgasbord of smiling faces,
secured with magnets,
overlapping,
shoulder to shoulder,
populates your refrigerator door
and charges your kitchen
with a cheer of celebration,
with a chorus
of unbridled moments,
with a spontaneous embrace
of youth and vigor
and pulsating pureness.

It is impossible to open
your refrigerator door
without optimism
for what's inside,
and, when it's open,
in the wide yawn
of its chilling mouth,
another explosion,
a cornucopia
of color and shape:
bottles, jars, little boxes,
and the natural groupings
of the bright parade of produce.

Your refrigerator is
the open hand of abundance,
the primal source of existence,
the unlimited hope and bounty
of repeated rejoicing,

the assurance of living,
and the brimming well of wellness.
It is the great fortune fully felt
by the ever-grateful soul
who seats me at her table and says,
"What can I get you to eat?"

Ode to your china cabinets

Glass cabinets,
mounted to the ceiling,
above the kitchen counter that separates
the dinner table from the kitchen,
your china seems weightless,
suspended in air,
waiting to be plucked
like porcelain fruit from a branch.

My love gathers her harvest,
plate, bowl, wine glass, glass,
filling her basket
with assorted shapes and sizes,
then arranges them, carefully,
in still-life patterns
on the canvas of the table.

And when her guests arrive,
she offers a meal and merriment
beneath the translucent branches,
beneath the shiny shade,
beneath the weightless canopy
of porcelain and crystal.

Ode to your dishwasher

After breakfast my love
takes her bowl and glass to wash them
in the small creek of the sink.
But after the well-attended dinner,
she takes the plates and pots and pans
to the mouth of the river.
She takes the stacked dishes
to the dishwasher.

Open jaw
with a hundred rubberized teeth,
with slots and baskets
to secure and carry
the porcelain, glass, and silver,
with wider molars below,
to clasp the clumsiness of pots and pans,
you are the receptacle that receives
the remnants of the day,
the basin that collects
whatever can be renewed,
whatever can be filled and used again.

You are the uncomplaining helper,
the ever-ready assistant,
who adds his watery voice
to the after-dinner conversation.
You are the waterfall
through which
each utensil passes
on its circular journey
from cabinet back to cabinet
and from drawer back to drawer.
You are the crystal pool
where the silverware swim,

shining their teeth and tails.
You are the pond where the pans
soak their water-lily leaves.

And, next morning,
you are emptied,
with a syncopated series of sounds,
with the opening and closing of cabinets,
with the swish and jingle of drawers,
with a clink and clank like the sound
of a knight storing a suit of armor.

Ode to the straightness of your back
as you sit at the table

I watch you sit at the table,
with straight back and soft shoulders,
talking to me, or typing,
or calling family on the phone.

Your manner and movement
immerse me in ease.

Your words and rhythm
encircle me in calm.

You sit patiently at the table,
with straight back and soft shoulders,
talking, typing,
or calling on the phone.

You will never believe
how beautiful you are.

Ode to the timer on your living-room lamp

The timer clicks and the light shines,
surprising you and me
in the shadows of early evening.

We've been talking for hours,
lost in the give and take
of speculation and opinion,
of debate and deliberation,
considering how to teach
and encourage imagination.
You've spoken with passion,
and I've spoken with passion,
and we've both played apologist
in order to more fully understand.

The world outside has continued,
unnoticed, slipping from day to dusk,
until the electric click
and sudden illumination.

Now it's time to turn
to evening endeavors—
a bite to eat, recalling
the day's pleasures,
the poem you'd like to read,
the song I'd like to sing,
the podcast we can listen to
together—a fresh procession
of uncounted hours
leading to preparing for bed,
to candlelight,
to unhurried embrace,
until we finally drift
to the kitchen for water.

Then the timer clicks off
and we're drenched in darkness,
except for the light
of the microwave clock,
recalling the world of hours
and confirming that it is,
in fact,
three o'clock in the morning.

Ode to my guitar in your living-room closet

Closed in your closet,
next to the vacuum,
leaning against the wall
with its head in the coats,
my guitar dutifully waits.

Hand-made guitar
of rosewood and cedar,
Spanish guitar that kissed you
with body vibration
and starry sound.

Each day it waits in silence,
remembering
the times it touched you.
It remembers
in the darkness,
beneath the coats, alone.

(But sometimes a Patagonia jacket
will rest a sleeve upon its shoulder).

Ode to the crown molding in your sunroom

I lie on the day bed in your sunroom
and gaze at the ceiling.
My eyes find and run the length
of the crown molding
atop the wall.
The flowing, smoothly sanded grooves,
the flawless paint,
and the perfectly cut angle
where two walls meet.

My eyes flow freely
from angle to angle
and from line to line,
savoring the sweep
and simplicity of shape,
the unblemished
lack of obstruction,
flowing
back and forth,
back and forth,
back and forth.

And the sun
through the western window
falls on the photographs
on the wall,
the photos of you,
your mother, and daughter,
and my eyes stray
from your photo
through the open door
to you,
at the table where you sit,
clicking keys,
sending signals
to warm the eyes and heart

of someone else clicking keys,
sending signals
from some other screen.

Then I fluff the pillow
behind my head
and let my eyes return
to the pleasure of the molding,
the rhythmic relaxation,
while my heart is warmed
by the sun,
the photographs,
and the certainty of the sound of you,
sending signals,
clicking keys of love,
in the next room.

Ode to a painting of a girl playing piano

I lie back on the loveseat and gaze
at a painting above the piano
of a girl playing piano.
Her back is to me,
and her piano is the same
as the piano beneath the painting.

The girl sits all day at her piano
and plays in silence.

Then my love sits down,
with her back to me,
at the piano beneath the painting,
and I suddenly hear
what the girl is playing.

Ode to your upright piano

Lonely piano,
waiting to be played,
I know what it feels like
to long for her touch,
to long for the feel
of her fingers upon you,
and long for her
to sit by your side
and share
the hours of the day.

There was a time
she worked
to know you better,
a time she pressed you
to sing for me.
It was a time of blossom
and growth,
a time of tenderness,
and the desire to please.

Sad piano,
don't be discouraged,
you know she knows
where you are
and what you offer,
you know she knows
the melodies you contain,
and she knows
that you are waiting,
and only has to decide
that today is the day
to sit down
and begin to play.

Ode to the dimmer switch on
your dining-room light

Dawn, mid-day, dusk:
with your dimmer switch
you create
any time at any time.

The evening begins
with the brightness of day,
with the table illuminated
by the full glow
of the dining-room light,
and it continues to burn
with its mid-day shine,
while you toil in the kitchen,
chopping and seasoning,
heating and cooling,
stirring and simmering
the evening dish,
but when the recipe is ready
and the plates reach the table,
the dazzling sun is dimmed
to a twilight tint that tempers,
that darkens and disguises
the objects of day.

Later, when the plates
are withdrawn
and the switch is dimmed anew,
your iPod plays a tune,
and we dance in the kitchen,
arm in arm,
in the gentle glow
of the electric moon.

Ode to your backpack by the door

Lightly filled backpack,
waiting by the door,
waiting to take its place among
the provisions in my van,
waiting to be transported
to pine-forest evenings
and mountain-morning streams,
you are the image of economy,
the essence of the one I love,
you are all my love needs,
when she distills her happy home
to its few essential things.

Simple backpack she carries
whenever she strays from home,
whether flying south to meet me,
or driving to watch the leaves,
you're the lightness of my love,
the incarnation of adaptability,
the endearing lack of excess
of a peaceful, uncomplaining heart.

My love is joyful and content
wherever she is and whatever she does.
She's modest, natural, and kind,
and as helpful and unassuming
as the simple pack she carries.

Ode to the quiet
in your neighborhood

The quiet
in your neighborhood
is a living quiet,
filled with regular,
consistent sounds,
and intermittent sounds
that accentuate
the quiet.

There is
just enough noise
to remind us
that we're living
in a living world,
but not enough
to distract us
when we're lost
in conversation.

I remember I heard
you complain
about the morning cars
that pass on the street,
and I was surprised,
not by the cars
that didn't bother me,
but because
I had so rarely
heard you complain.

Ode to the breeze through
your kitchen window

Without opening my eyes
I know the time and the season.
The breeze through your kitchen window
is the daily messenger
of continuity and change.

The June day was lived
with re-conditioned air,
with artificial currents
cooled and recycled,
but now it fills
with unaltered breath,
with sounds, smells,
and temperature from the yard,
with freshness flowing in.

Your kitchen window
is the half-opened door
that connects inside to out,
the invitation
for invisible movement
to take a turn
around the house,
transporting aromas
of meals, plants,
soaps, and shampoos
from room to room.
It brings distant sounds near:
the crack of thunder,
the whisper of leaves,
the chorus of crickets.

Your kitchen window admits
the first kiss of spring
and the last kiss of autumn,
the exhilaration of rain,
and the breath
of thirst-quenched soil.

In the dying light I recline
on the bed in your sunroom,
when suddenly the breeze brings me
the scent of your hair
after an evening bath,
and I follow its trail
as you glide about the house,
pleasing, soothing, settling
the remnants of day,
discharging chores,
ordering countertops,
washing a dish or utensil,
opening a cabinet
and retrieving linens,
building a nest
for the shared journey
of sleep.

Like the breeze,
you give motion to my life,
and when I notice a sudden freshness,
a loving touch upon my skin,
I don't know without opening my eyes
if it's you,
or the fingers of the breeze,
that I feel.

Ode to the keyboard of your laptop

Symbol-keyed
laptop piano,
playing silent melodies
in the imagination
of sender and receiver,
combining typeface tones
to create colors, shapes, and stories
in the deciphering mind:
sights, smells, and contact,
brought to life in the act
of writing and reading.

My love sits at her instrument,
composing symphonies,
orchestrating
introductory overtures,
sugary second movements,
and cheerful conclusions with codas
that repeat and reassure.

The melodies she plays
on her alphabetic piano
strike chords of a more loving world,
playful chords that sing
the joy of imagination,
the kiss of compassion,
and the celebration of equity.

My love sits down
to the possibilities of her laptop
like a child sits down
to her toy piano.

Ode to you watering your plants

I watch you drift
from room to room
with your rain-cloud spout,
dispersing showers
on the thirst of potted plants,
fulfilling your fertile destiny
as dutiful Demeter,
coaxing leaves and blossoms
from seeds and soil.

Your house breathes
like an arboretum,
a grateful greenhouse
with jungle corners
and countertop bowers,
a mini-Arcadia
of growing shape and color,
thriving
under the loving hand
of its garden goddess.

Ode to your bed

The evening flows in
through the windows,
and you go to your bed
to journey through the night.

Ship of dreams
and candlelight voyage,
sailing under starry skies,
your bed is where you go
to give yourself,
unguarded and exposed,
to your lover,
or to sheltering sleep.

Your high, sturdy bed
remains unchanged,
night after night,
standing on its sturdy legs,
while you shift and alter,
determining who
it will hold tonight.
Will you bring it passion or peace?
Insomnia or repose?
Will you emerge restless or rested,
anxious or at ease?

Sometimes your bed
is a valley in bloom,
with soft grass and flowers,
and other times it's a beach.
Your sheets are the waves
of a warm ocean
that rock you to sleep.

On those fortunate nights
when we go to sleep together,

the same bed that supports us
carries us through different
journeys and dreams,
and you wake, from time to time,
to listen to me breathe.

And when the morning finally comes,
and I wake and reach out
to find your familiar form,
I discover you're already up,
already dressed and at the table,
typing out hellos
to greet the new day.

Ode to a starry night

The goal is to have
starry nights
under starry nights,
to live in a sea with no surface,
with currents
circling upon currents.

We discovered that the universe
is a reflexive verb.

And the verb is like living
in an undiscovered country,
language, body, emotional field,
and becoming
the rhythm, waves, and breeze,
without knowing.

Like having been everywhere forever.

Ode to the smell of microwaved egg

There is a morning aroma
without which my overnight stay
is utterly incomplete,
a sweet fragrance
that fills the house,
an insistent odor that lingers
after the source has succumbed,
after the seasoned dish
has been devoured.

It is the smell that announces
the dawn of a new day,
the perfume that permeates,
emanates from the kitchen,
it is the pungent blossom
I cannot help but inhale
when my love pushes a button
and microwaves an egg for breakfast.

Simple sustenance,
cooked in a small bowl
and consumed
as part of a simple repast,
life-giving edible that feeds
the mind, body, and limbs
that I love to love,
essential essence that becomes
the woman I adore,
the breathing being I touch,
and who touches me.

Before rising,
in bed, half asleep,
I smell the aroma

drift through
the bedroom door,
and I relax,
I am calm and contented,
I'm at peace,
because I know
that my love will be well,
I know she'll be satisfied
and sustained,
I know she'll be nourished
for another day.

Ode to the sound of the furnace in winter

As the snow piles up outside,
we lie in bed and talk.

A streetlight illuminates the flakes
that brighten the bedroom window.

We pull the covers to our chins
and turn our heads to the flakes.

The room beyond the covers
grows cold until a low rumble
adds its voice to our voice.

We snuggle even more warmly
into the covers and watch the flakes
shine through the window.

You turn to me and say,
"Lucky me, lucky you, lucky us!"

Ode to the little girl's eyes

The little girl's eyes,
drinking in
the sweep and scope
of the horizon,
the level extension of fields,
the South Dakota glow
on shimmering color
at dawn and dusk,
the blue, silver, and gold
in the grasses.

The young girl's eyes,
shining out
beneath the woolen cap,
above the fur collar,
bright eyes, playing,
laughing with other girls,
running with friends
in dresses, barelegged,
through the sub-zero air.

The assessing eyes
in the schoolhouse,
observing the teacher,
considering, questioning,
knowing there must be
a better way
to encourage and inspire.

The expectant eyes,
anticipating the newness
of predictable things,
the sequence of seasons,

the fertile journey from
leaf to snow, seed to flower.

The accustomed eyes,
reassured by familiar
sights and structures:
the faces of parents,
siblings, friends,
the church and schoolhouse,
the drugstore, grocery,
streets and street corners,
the houses, hospital,
bank, and parks,
the summers on the lake
with celebration and sport,
the summers at the ranch
with sweat and slowness,
the stretching afternoons
with bugs in the air,
the slumbering mornings
with bugs on the ground.

In your bedroom you built
a personal home,
constructing in your corner
a sanctuary of sights,
a microcosm of assurance,
a festival of items
—cups, bottles, binders,
photographs, figures, and magazines—
from your father's store.

(Your eyes watched him at work,
studied and admired him,

then watched him years later
when his pain turned to stupor
beneath a morphine drip,
and later when your secrets
—private moments
and consoling conversations—
were laid to rest
when he closed his eyes.)

Loving, caring eyes,
of the woman now,
that hoped, wondered,
wept, and shone
when they saw themselves
reflected, for the first time,
in your daughter's eyes.

Unchanging eyes,
gazing in the mirror
at the changing face,
with the same hope and wonder
of the little girl's eyes.

Ode to the goodness of your heart

Loving heart,
made of pain and hope
and reverence and sorrow,
made of attention
to others,
of outward focus,
of observing and discerning
who is in need
and what can be done.

Giving heart,
shaping solutions,
large and small,
to simple
and life-changing problems.

Open heart that understands
that the way to feel love
is by loving.

Each day is an itinerary
of scheduled
and spontaneous stops,
of thoughtful notes,
letters, and calls,
of reaching out,
and sacrificing sleep
until every loved one
feels loved,
until the day
has been put to rest,
with a plan
for a better tomorrow.

Ode to your Christmas decorations on the mantel

Idealized image of home,
simple pattern from a simple time,
school, drugstore, house, hotel,
buildings that softly shine.
It's a world of imagination
from the heart of the little girl,
who lives within the woman
that arranged this loving world.

I sit back in my chair,
and you sit back in yours,
admiring the invented village,
its bright windows and bright doors.

(The flicker of electric candles
moves the skaters on the pond,
and the cotton among the trees
makes us glad we're safe and warm).

It's a setting of wished-for scenes,
built on love and being kind,
where people help each other,
and are glad to share their time.

You've spent your year in meetings,
in classrooms and county halls,
fighting to help the schools
break down dividing walls,
but tonight you'll go with me,
on a journey through your town,
hand in hand through imagination,
beneath its starry crown.

I sit back in my chair,
and you sit back in yours,

admiring the invented village,
its bright windows and bright doors.

And tomorrow we'll sit down
with the Grinch and Charlie Brown!

Ode to the absence of black and white

"I don't deal in black and white,"
you said,
and a sliver of light
sliced the gloom
and kissed my hopeless heart.

The day was damp with snow,
and melting snow,
and my heart cried out for air.

I was where you had been,
before I found what was lost
in the middle of what was lost,
before I could say the words
that I had always felt,
words I had said repeatedly
with everything but words.

You could never say never,
you said,
and those words were a light
streaming from a lighthouse
across a rocky shore,
a hope to hang on to,
a flickering fire
to save my life.

Ode to the feeling of shelter

We sat in the car, holding hands,
beneath the flutter of autumn leaves,
and it felt shelter.

We walked slowly, in the sun,
through the cool canyon air,
and it felt shelter.

You shared a triumph from your classroom,
of love and understanding,
and it felt shelter.

You looked up from your grading,
and smiled when my email arrived,
and it felt shelter.

You drifted drowsy, through my songs,
wrapped warmly in your chair,
and it felt shelter.

We faced the news that shook us,
and soothed each other's pain,
and it felt shelter.

Through courageous conversation
we made our honest way,
and it felt shelter.

At the grave I took your hand,
and read my mother's name,
and it felt shelter.

You spoke of perfect kindness,
and a future we could share,
and it felt shelter.

A song

I know you are threadbare and worn
with the weary strike of iron
ringing the notes in your name,

and even the tireless minstrel
is tired of his own insistence
on solitude's graceless strain,

yet it had been enough,
and the mournful sounds a song,

had we but moved without motion
in motion through the dawn.

Day is done

Now the day is done
and all that has been lived
passes slowly to shadow,
all the kisses and conversations,
hellos and good-byes,
and evidence of a life once lived.

And all our efforts to stop the flow
from one minute to the next,
our search for assurance
of a shared tomorrow,
wind vacantly down to this:

an empty street viewed
through a picture window,

no moving or living thing,

the light of a streetlamp
illuminating the empty street.

Made in the USA
Columbia, SC
26 September 2020